Our Journey with Anorexia

CW00454874

Ruth Steggles

Our Journey with Anorexia How a Parent Can Be Part of Their Child's Recovery

By Ruth Steggles
with Contributions from Katharine and Gareth Steggles

Our Journey with Anorexia

Dedication

This book is written with love for all my immediate family, for Gareth and William who stood by and supported us during this difficult time, but mostly for Katharine because it was her strength and resilience that got us through.

Today, as I was going through notes writing whilst writing this book, I came across a letter Katharine wrote to us when she was very ill. It read, "I am really sorry about this evening....What happens is I get annoyed with myself for causing everyone aggro, but then I take that out on you which just makes me feel worse because I want to make everyone happy and I want to be someone you and Dad can be proud of...." Katharine, I want you to know that we could not be more proud of you in any way. This hasn't been a journey that any of us would have chosen, but we have all learnt so much. You have shown us how amazing you are. You have achieved so much and learnt to live with the perfect imperfection that you are. You are strong, incredible and awesome. We love you so much and I am truly grateful for everything you have taught us.

Our Journey with Anorexia

Acknowledgements

As a family we want to say a huge thank you to the support we had from school, particularly to the amazing Caz Atkins who works incredibly hard and has a true gift as a teacher in the way she cares for and looks out for her pupils.

I need to say a personal and massive thank you to Bill, the amazing nurse who sat and listened to me every week, holding a space for me and helping me have the courage to cope. Bill you made me feel safe and helped me believe it would all be ok.

Thanks to Kevin Burch and Diba, for suggesting I had to do this work. To my amazing friend Alex Brown for introducing me to these two, and believing in me always, for giving me courage to be who I need to be. Everyone needs a mad crazy friend like you!

Thanks to my good friends who agreed to read this for me and keep me on the right track: Karen Morgan, Karen Alston, Michelle Clarke and Linda Perry; thank you for your time when life is so busy.
Thank you to Jaqui Malpass, my book coach, who got me started and kept me on track. And without whom I would have had no idea how to begin.

Finally, to all our friends and family who stood by us through this difficult time and did whatever they could do.

Ruth Steggles

Introduction

Our daughter, Katharine, developed anorexia under our noses without us even realising. She was the "perfect" daughter; clever, thoughtful and hard working. Then, one Easter, she ate a single, tiny piece of Easter egg and declared she was full. I looked at her, saw how thin she was and realised how little I had seen her eat in the last week. That was the start of our terrifying journey. We battled to get the right medical support but what little there was she refused to work with. I had no choice but to scour the internet and find whatever help and advice I could to help me save her. Always at the back of my mind was the knowledge that young girls die of anorexia - but I was going to do everything I could to make sure that didn't happen to our daughter!

When Katharine's illness started I had been coaching in my direct selling business for 10 years and had done a lot of reading about self-development, which gave me some resources to draw on, but I was still pretty lost as to what to do. Eventually I found what we needed and after a period of intensive work she began to see her value again and regain her wish to survive. She is now once again healthy, happy and thriving. I know what it feels like to be terrified for your child. I know how scared and confused everyone in the family is. I know how the stress and tension from one meal time stretches into the next, and how socially isolated you can become as a result. I saw how lost and lonely an anorexia sufferer can feel.

I am writing this from a mother's perspective; I am claiming only to be an authority on our family, and our family dynamic, no more. What I write about here worked for us and I am hoping that it will help you by giving you some ideas that might help you. Whilst writing I was encouraged to put in technical evidence to support what I was saying, but when I went back to look at the books I found so hard to read when Katharine was ill, I found them full of technical references. I list the books that I read in the resources. If you want the technical stuff I recommend you go there. I can now read them and find them intellectually interesting, but it wasn't what I wanted when I was where you are now. I wanted something I could do today that gave me hope. My aim in writing this book is that you too can find the hope and resources to help your child through to an even healthier place than before their illness. This is the book that I couldn't find when I knew that I wanted to help Katharine. In this book I have brought together into one place all the information I wanted and all the techniques I used.

WHO IS THIS BOOK FOR?
This book is written for the parents of a child suffering with anorexia. Katharine was twelve when she was diagnosed and so what I write about is the experience with a child that age. Having talked to other people I believe the techniques we used are relevant for many adolescents going through a tough time mentally or emotionally.

It may also be of interest to anyone who has a friend or relative with anorexia, and for anyone suffering with anorexia it may give you some ideas as to things that may help you or the people around you.

WHY THIS BOOK IS IMPORTANT
I have written this so that you may not feel quite so alone; so that you may find someone who identifies with some of your feelings; so that you have more resources to get through this difficult time; so that you can be a significant part of your child's recovery and so you too can make anorexia part of your history rather than part of your daily life. This is a book to give you courage, confidence, hope and skills.

HOW TO USE THIS BOOK
For simplicity i have split this book into two parts:

Part One is the story of our family; me, Ruth (42 when it started), my husband Gareth (46), our son William (14) and our daughter Katharine (12), what we went through and how we came out the other end. This is certainly not essential reading; it sets the scene and explains what happened to us.

Part Two describes the steps that we took to help Katharine recover. I hope that it will give you ideas to help your child start on the road to recovery. I am sorry to say I am offering you no magic spell or quick fix, but what I am offering are the ideas and skills that helped me to help Katharine.

If you are keen to get into what you can do today to make a difference for your child, you may want to go straight to Part Two.

KATHARINE'S VOICE

When it was first suggested that I write this book it was important for me that Katharine was ok with it, which she was. She had thought that she would write part of it, but has been so busy having a good time and living her life that she hasn't contributed as much as she had originally intended. She has however written a few things that occurred to her and felt important to say. I have included these in italics at points where they seemed relevant. They are her unedited voice.

HOW THIS BOOK CAME ABOUT

So why am I here? why write this book? After the experience of coming through anorexia as a family, and having coached in my own business prior to Katharine's illness, I decided to get a formal qualification and set up a coaching business. This was going really well; I was loving what I did and everything I had done over the last 15 years, including all the work I had done with katharine, helped form my philosophies and practice. then one day a friend introduced me to another coach (working with teenagers with confidence issues) and his gp girl-friend. I was quite in awe of their abilities and during the conversation katharine's illness came up. I discovered whilst talking to these two experts that I was telling them things they weren't aware of. They were really shocked that I wasn't coaching teenage girls with anorexia. When they suggested this is what I should do I felt sick to my core and absolutely terrified. it had just never occurred to me that I had valuable experience that could help other people who were going through what we had been through. And the whole thing was still so raw! Whilst on the one hand katharine's illness feels like a life-time ago, in actual fact we are probably only 18 months clear. then all my own issues about not being good enough came up, and what if what I did with katharine didn't work for other people, and so on. Then I realised that when I was where you are now, all I wanted was something to clutch on to. To me, doing something was always better than doing nothing, apart from waiting until the next appointment or meeting and desperately hoping for a ray of light at the next weigh-in (with katharine dreading it and being terrified of the outcome - either too much or too little weight gain). I needed to believe that one day this would all be a thing of the past. So I scoured the internet to find any information that could help me. There were a handful of books written by professionals, which to me felt like they were for professionals. They were cold and clinical. The one book that really offered me some hope was written by another mother whose daughter had been in a very bad way, and for much longer than we had experienced. She gave me some techniques that i believe helped me to help katharine. Since then, the tools that I have discovered through my coaching have added to the range of skills, thoughts and ideas that I now have.

IMPERFECTION
Each time I read this book there are things I think I could have said better or slightly differently things I could expand on or reduce. It is however more important to me to get this in your hands so that you can start on your journey to recovery for your daughter, than to spend the next six months trying to produce something more perfect. So please forgive the imperfections and read this in the spirit that it is written. I want you to start thinking and exploring yourself, I want you to be part of your child's recovery, I want you to take courage and know you are enough!

HOW I FELT
So, before I start, I want to tell you how I felt, which may not be exactly the same as how you are feeling right now but I suspect that you are not feeling great! I was terrified! I knew that there was something seriously wrong a long time before any professional would put a name to it. Obviously I knew that anorexia existed but not in my family and not in my experience; that was in families with problems or issues. We were just a regular, normal, happy family. People around me offered a few platitudes of, "I am sure it will be fine," but I had already started reading whatever I could. And I already knew that it wasn't always fine and that children, and adults, died from this illness. There were also long term

health implications and some people didn't recover; they just lived with it. I veered from thinking that this wasn't going to happen to our daughter to a feeling of complete devastation. I was scared and desperate, but I was prepared to fight and do whatever it took to find Katharine the help she needed. My feelings at the time also incorporated grief; the beautiful talented daughter we had loved for the last eleven and a half years appeared to have left us, and I wasn't sure we were going to get her back. If you feel any of these things or anything similar I want you to know that it doesn't have to stay this way. In this book you will find skills that will enable you to make these feelings and this experience a thing of the past.

SOME HOPE

This morning Katharine sat across the table from me; stunningly beautiful, full of vitality, everything she was before her illness and much more. There really is hope. For us it wasn't easy - I don't imagine this illness can be - it was exhausting and draining. It affected not just our immediate family but our extended family as well; it made socialising with our friends hard and time seemed to go in slow motion. In an attempt to have some sort or normality, we experienced the worst holiday of our lives. A couple of places will remain off my go-to list for ever due to the horrible memories they bring back. But, in the almost two years since, we have had wonderful times once more and Katharine and I are closer than ever before.

Contents

Ruth Steggles

Part 1

Our Story

Ruth Steggles

Chapter 1

From Top to Bottom in 12 Months

"Transformation is a process, and as life happens there are tons of ups and downs. It's a journey of discovery – there are moments on mountaintops and moments in deep valleys of despair."

Rick Warren

Ruth Steggles

GREAT TIMES (THE TOP)

2009 was a brilliant year for us as a family. My business was flying, our son William had at last seemed to settle in to secondary school and Katharine was doing really well in her final year at primary school. We felt settled and happy. On a bit of a whim we decided to fulfil our ambition of taking the children to Disneyland Florida. It was brilliant! Our biggest challenge was getting William out of bed in the mornings but the copious photos of that year show an extremely happy family. We felt as if we were living the dream!

Katharine was the perfect daughter. She was self-contained, high achieving, organised, helpful, attractive and fun to be with. At primary school she excelled in everything except PE, which her form tutor made a particular point of stating (I think for the sake of everyone else in the class, because it was evident that Katharine was really able). I can honestly say we had never had it so good and I have never been happier. To us as parents there seemed no reason to worry about the transition to secondary school, as Katharine was academic, sociable and popular. That summer I persuaded her to start jogging with me for fun and all was good with the world.

STARTING SECONDARY SCHOOL

Secondary school started well and Katharine had some nice friends. In the October of that year Katharine had a dental brace fitted and I remember the dental nurse saying, "Now, you want to be careful that the boys don't see you with food in your brace!" It wasn't until six months later that I realised how that throw-away comment was pivotal. Now, I can look back and recognise that as the moment that Katharine stopped snacking and eating between meals, but at the time I was oblivious to the subtle changes taking place. Christmas came and went and Katharine was looking great, I hadn't noticed at all that she was looking slimmer. My in-laws tell me now that when they saw her that Christmas they thought she was looking a bit too thin.

Katharine had continued running; now much faster than me, she mostly went on her own - and she seemed happy. I guess her body shape was changing but that all seemed perfectly normal. She did tell me much later that, about this time, a few people had complemented her on looking good and she liked that feeling, along with the slight weight loss. A couple of weeks before Easter I noticed how little she was taking to school for lunch. I reflected on when she had last eaten a yoghurt, something that had previously been a staple of her diet. My senses were suddenly on full alert. I spoke to a couple of friends, one of whom was a GP. They tried to reassure me and cautioned me to not panic.

"I couldn't say when I first had this growth in my mind, or when it started taking over completely, I don't think I could put it down to one factor. I know that I was unhappy at school, I felt all those things that I'm sure most girls feel at some point during their teenage years; ugly, fat, lonely. During this time I had found a sport that I could actually do…better than other people. I relished this; I had never felt sporty at all, quite the opposite. I began running more and more and it felt good; even better when I started losing weight. I guess it was just a downwards spiral from there. Food and exercise were something I could control in my life, something that gave me a sense of achievement. At first it was to become as healthy as possible; and this was the thought that the anorexia drew on throughout. "I need to exercise to be healthy", "I can't eat that it's unhealthy." In my illogical mind, the thought that, "if I eat that it will make me fat" made perfect sense. Maybe if I could lose just a bit more weight and trained a bit more, I would feel better about myself; I would feel attractive."

RED ALERT (THE BOTTOM)
On the run up to Easter, we had all been having the usual playful banter about whether or not we would buy the children Easter eggs and what their favourite variety would be. Katharine was as engaged in that conversation as ever. On Easter morning, among the excitement of the moment, I clearly remember Katharine breaking off a centimetre square

of her egg, eating it with pleasure and then declaring she was full! Up till eight months previously, Katharine had been our sausage and chip eating, chocolate loving daughter. My emotions went into freefall: I now knew that something was seriously wrong. That was the moment that my world temporarily stopped. It stopped being bright and bubbly and happy. It suddenly went from fast, colourful and exciting, to grey, scary and slow. It was in that moment, with that sudden change of tempo, that I immediately knew we had a big problem!

"The first real confrontation about food I remember was Easter day. We had family friends staying over and I remember my parents urging me to eat more food, causing a fuss. I desperately wanted them to shut up, it was excruciatingly embarrassing for me; nothing was wrong with me, why were they making such a scene? But when they asked me to eat something more, I couldn't do it, there was no question about it, I just could not eat a piece of toast; I would rather suffer the argument. So the rowing started, and it was horrible. I was so embarrassed by it all, the fact that everyone thought I had an issue around food was so stupid, I hated it and refused to accept it. I remember begging my mum to please be quiet because our friends would notice. Embarrassment seems to be a common theme with anorexia. There were countless occasions where a public scene would occur and everyone would be embarrassed, ashamed even. But why should anorexia be something to be embarrassed about? It's something you learn, only by experience. It is an illness that is perceived so negatively."

My first step was to take Katharine to our GP. He was lovely and talked to Katharine about why I might have concerns. She denied there was any sort of problem, but the GP thought it would be a good idea to refer her, just to check it all out. He referred us to CAMHS (Child and Adolescent Mental Health Service). As we waited, things seemed to spiral. Our acknowledgement that we were concerned seemed to make matters much worse. It is possible that it was just my awareness that had changed, but I worried that the steps I had taken had exacerbated the situation. Katharine wanted to cook and plan food. She talked about food all the time. Without the understanding that I later gained, that this obsession was a by-product of her starving herself, it did produce a smoke screen to my concerns. I guess at that point I thought that we would get some professional help and our problem would be in safe hands; someone would provide an answer, Katharine would get better and it would all be ok. I can't remember exactly when the real fear set in but this was the beginning of our waiting game...

Chapter 2

Empty Rooms and Squidgy Chairs

"No one ever told me that grief felt so like fear."

C.S. Lewis, A Grief Observed

Ruth Steggles

THE PROCESS STARTS

So at last, three weeks later, we had an appointment with CAMHS (Child & Adolescent Mental Health Service). We met with a doctor and we explained our concerns exactly as we had before, whilst Katharine sat in a stony silence not wishing to be spoken to or to respond. We couldn't be given a diagnosis because, as I was told later, in order to be diagnosed with anorexia the team first had to see a specific weight loss over a specific time period. In hindsight, the need to let a disease get worse before it can be labelled seems bonkers to me! So we were put on a list to see a dietician and sent away to see what happened. A couple of weeks later, the dietician sat us down and explained the make-up of a healthy diet, and what Katharine should be looking to eat every day. She was lovely and I found it reassuring to be told what I already thought to be the case.

We had entered a cycle of waiting rooms with dim lights, Katharine sitting tensely, followed by consulting rooms with squidgy chairs and a box of tissues. Every consultation was preceded by the stress of Katharine standing on the scales in a little dark annex room to be weighed.

Meanwhile, outside the temporary reassurance of a professional's office, things seemed to be rapidly escalating. We felt a need to supervise Katharine eating and, needless to say, this was a battle she didn't like; we didn't enjoy it either. As I tried to get up to join her for breakfast, her wake-up time became earlier and earlier. She told me she just couldn't sleep. Once she hit the 5am slot I had to draw the conclusion that I needed to sleep in order to face the day. So I had to trust that she was eating her breakfast (previously her favourite meal of the day) and took the bowl by the side of the sink, with a dribble of milk left in the bottom, as the evidence I so desperately wanted that she was eating. I could see that she was losing weight rapidly now. It was bizarre to feel that at least she had now lost enough weight to have a diagnosis! This enabled me to talk to her school about the situation. They were exceptionally supportive, particularly of her brother, William.

I can't really tell now what was "Will's own stuff," and how much of his misery at the time was related to the stress and tension at home. I know that there were issues among his friendship group, and he was wrestling with his own feelings and the grief we were going through as a family. Grief was a really strong emotion for me that Summer. Where had our beautiful, honest, sparkly daughter gone? We used to laugh with her so much and now everything was grey - would she ever come back?

Our world had cracked apart. Gareth and William struggled to come to terms with what was going on; it was hard for them not to be angry when Katharine fussed over what she was prepared to eat. Meal times were tense and stressful.

I obviously knew that this kind of thing happened, but in other people's lives, not ours! Life slowed down and took on a surreal feel. Katharine became all that mattered, everything else seemed to fade into the background, and we waited…..

LOOKING FOR ANSWERS

I have always been a solution orientated person, so when there was a problem I needed to take action. I bought the first book about anorexia in April. It was cold, clinical and horrific! This was definitely what "other people went through." As Katharine began to get skinnier and her bones began to protrude, the hair on her head began to fall out as the hair on her body started to increase. This seemed so unfair for a young girl concerned about her appearance. We tried to carry on some sort of normality, but soon discovered that all our socialising had revolved around eating in some way, and it was just so hard to be with other people when all our concerns were with Katharine. We tried a couple of parties with friends, but it just felt too much like hard work, she was always uncomfortable and unhappy and so it made it miserable for everyone else. We just stopped planning things in our diary – it was easier that way. We started existing rather than living.

FEELINGS

During this time I was flooded with a range of emotions. Once I had started reading about anorexia I was more scared than ever. I was hearing that people die of it, or never recover living with it as a constant part of their lives. I was suffering huge grief for the daughter we had lost; would we ever get her back? And if we didn't I wasn't sure what the biggest horror would be - her dying or her being anorexic for ever. I rolled through these thoughts regularly. I suspect I was very dull company at the time.

I don't remember thinking about anything other than Katharine. I remember going to a meeting for work and asking the speaker what he knew about anorexia. I was totally absorbed in what we were going through and trying to find anything that could help. I was frustrated that other people didn't understand, and I was conscious that one or two people blamed Katharine or us. There was no reason anyone else should understand, we didn't; but it often made conversation with other people stilted. When others asked how we were what I really wanted to say was "shit actually," but I just pretended. I was finding whatever books I could on the subject. They seemed to be few and far between. What I did get seemed dry and inconclusive. They told me what I might expect to happen, that this was a serious illness and that regaining a safe weight was critical. I got that Katharine needed to eat more and regain weight; that was just proving a tireless daily battle. Trying to support her against her fear, reassure her and provide some sort of semblance of normality for the rest of the family was exhausting.

Katharine continued to lose weight; our day lurched from one meal time to the next and then the next. Interspersed with long conversations with Katharine, who was scared most of the time. She needed to talk often. Wracked with fear and guilt. She cried a lot, we talked a lot. We negotiated constantly about what sport she could do if she ate certain things. The professionals were keen to take all exercise away as soon as possible, but our nurses seemed to understand the need for Katharine to get the head space she got when she ran. Allowing her some exercise meant she was prepared to eat some things. Now it seems absolutely mad looking back on it, but during this time Katharine competed in a couple of track races. It was horrible to see her run. She was so thin. There was no way she could compete at her best. I remember watching other parents cheering their children on, wanting them to do well. Every race she ran I just wanted her to complete it, get it over with, survive it. She worried before every race, was determined to do it and I was just hugely relieved every time they were over, even though it meant engaging in the conversation with her anxiety about how she performed. The whole thing was an emotional ordeal for both of us. My husband and I would sometimes see who drew the short straw to accompany her and the inevitable dark moods. Often I wanted to be there just because I was scared and felt a need to protect her, despite the round of conversations I knew we would have.

Katharine managed to stay in school and her year head and other staff were very supportive. Katharine was determined that no-one else should realise there was a problem. I have no idea what her immediate friendship group thought; I suspect other people must have seen there was something horribly wrong.

THE TEAM

By this time we were assigned a team. My memories are mostly of the waiting room and the weighing scales. Katharine saw a psychologist on her own, to whom she apparently refused to speak. The only light relief to that was that I got to talk to someone else on my own, and whilst I rarely came away with more than a tiny glimmer of a hope or an idea to try, the process of off-loading and being in a safe place for a short while was huge. The worst appointment was a family session we had. It took some persuasion to get Katharine, William and Gareth to agree to going. They sat in silence whilst I engaged with the facilitator. Everyone else was so relieved to get out of that room; it was a process never to be repeated. The one moment of agreement through that stretch of time was that no-one wanted to do that again. It heightened Katharine's sense of guilt and the boys just felt truly uncomfortable.

"The family mentoring session for me was vaguely positive. Whereas my mum had read and researched enough to understand what was going on for me, I knew the boys couldn't comprehend at all what I was doing. I felt, the longer I acted the way I was acting, the further I grew apart from them, I didn't blame them for any dislike they felt

towards me for putting them through it. I hated how distanced we all were; we had always been a close family, but not in a "family mentoring" type way. I know we were all dreading the session, but Mum was adamant about trying any methods possible that could be helpful. The hour was painful and awkward, as expected; again I felt terrible guilt for bringing them to this point. However, I left with the sense that the boys had a greater understanding of what I was going through. Maybe they could see why I continued to struggle against the medical help provided, that I wasn't just being uncooperative; how patronised and undermined I felt."

Katharine still refused to talk to the psychologist that had been assigned to her. We graduated from the CAMHS team to the CIT team (Crisis Intervention Team), which meant that Katharine had a nurse assigned to her and I had one assigned to me. Katharine went out for lunch with her nurse once a week, and I had an hour to off load with a nurse on my own. The nursing team we had was the most useful part of the support we got. For me, a weekly session when I could just talk about my worries and my fears, helped me to keep myself together enough to be able to try and support Katharine through the week. Katharine's own nurse was young and attractive; she seemed to get on with her very well in the beginning. For me the respite of having someone else looking after her for a short period of time was absolutely huge. It was by now Summer time and the picture I now have in my mind of Katharine at that time is her dressed in a big baggy sweat shirt, a scarf and gloves, frozen the entire time.

"I was never happy to talk to anyone from the various medical teams who knew me from their various "BMI" charts. At first this was because they didn't understand that I just wasn't anorexic, and then gradually as I became more acceptant of this, the sessions I had felt more and more patronising. None of them knew me, why would they

understand what I was going through! When I was put onto a more specialised team, I was assigned someone who would take me out of school at a lunchtime every now and again. This was a welcome prospect to me as I couldn't stand lunchtimes in school. Lunchtimes were cold, lonely and painful experiences at this point in my life. Quite often I would be alone, as I couldn't stand outside for more than a few minutes in the unbearable temperatures. I picked at food, creating weird rules in my head for what was and wasn't acceptable to eat; I don't like to think what people thought of me. So being taken out was a treat, a novelty I looked forward to. The conversation I put up with, because I had to. In hindsight I think these sessions did help me slightly, because I knew I had to talk to be able to leave school on these occasions, I did talk. This did help to an extent. I realise now how lucky I was to have someone I could talk to at home, whenever I needed, who really understood every moment of pain that I went through; who wasn't getting paid to read my details off of a chart."

After a second visit to the dietician we agreed that it may be worth Katharine taking some Ensure (A nutritional milkshake drink) to help maintain her weight. She agreed to this as it was a known calorific value and so in the scheme of things felt relatively safe to her.

IN NEED OF MORE HELP
It was around this time that I realised that waiting for the professionals to sort things out wasn't necessarily going to give us the answers and solutions I wanted as quickly as I wanted them. I read a couple more books but I wasn't finding things that resonated with me or empowered me in any way to make me feel like I could make a difference. They were about coping and maintenance, I didn't want to stay here; I wanted my daughter back and I was scared.

The books I had read had warned me about some of the experiences to be expected, like the light downy hair growing on Katharine's body in a futile attempt to protect her. When the hair on her head started falling out in handfuls it seemed the last insult to injury. She was more obsessed than ever about clothes, and finding things that she looked good in was harder than ever. Where had our vibrant funny daughter gone? She was constantly scared and secretive.

Time around the dinner table was tense. Before anorexia we used to chat and laugh and listen to music. Now there was mostly a strained silence, with me occasionally trying to find a neutral topic of conversation to ease the gloom. Some days she obviously enjoyed her Ensure drinks, accepting that she should drink them and they were good for her. She allowed herself the pleasure of consuming something, but on other days particularly if she was about to weigh or had been weighed her fear and torment came to the surface and she needed calming and to be persuaded to have them.

I understood that our support team wanted to see some weight gain before they pushed for further psychological intervention (not that I was convinced she would talk to anyone else), but to me it all seemed so slow. Katharine was at that time just skirting the possibility of needing to go into hospital. I was so frightened about her going into hospital. I didn't want her to start associating with other anorexics and end up becoming even better at being an anorexic. I was already aware that she could get good at whatever she chose to and her state of mind at that moment could have sparked a desire to perfect her starving even more. One of my points of relief at the time was that she hadn't made herself sick. I always made sure that I stayed with her for at least half an hour after meal times to reduce that possibility. I also knew how much she hated being sick and that if she chose that path we had gone to another level.

Ruth Steggles

Chapter 3

Something to Work with and the Holiday from Hell

"Hope is being able to see that there is light despite all of the darkness."

Desmond Tutu

Ruth Steggles

SOMETHING TO WORK WITH

During my regular internet searches, I came across a mother whose daughter had been severely ill with anorexia and had been hospitalised on several occasions. She had reached the depths of despair before she came across the understanding that the brain can be trained to respond differently. Her book, Mom Please Help, spends a lot of time talking about neuro-plasticity and how changing the conversations we have, the language we use and the emotions in the environment, can change the way that someone thinks. The real pivotal thing for me was a game, which I will explain in the second part of the book, called "Who Are You?" What this game did was introduce some hope. It helped to focus on the future and over time made a difference.

Since my first realisation of Katharine's illness, I had constantly been asking myself questions and seeking answers. I attended every meeting with a professional with a scribbled list of things I wanted to know. It amazed me that even though my questions seemed clear to me, the answers I came away with were often vague and inconclusive. Around this time I started using the Mom Please Help book to plan what things I wanted to try with Katharine. I started looking at strategies I could introduce in an attempt to help her.

Throughout the whole period, one of the things we had done was to walk together. This was always a great way to spend time. Sometimes we just walked and sometimes it was a really useful time to talk. Going for a walk is a calming process; after a few minutes we got into a smooth rhythm and talking became easier. It was while walking on the hill near our home that Katharine was often able to open up about the things she was scared of.

We started playing the "Who Are You?" game. When I first asked her who she was she had absolutely nothing to say. It was heart breaking. But every day for about half an hour we would play the game and, over the next few months, painstakingly slowly, I started to see a difference in how Katharine was thinking.

TIME FOR A HOLIDAY

Meanwhile, we were supposed to be going on holiday. Gareth's parents have a place in Spain and we hadn't visited for a long time. We had planned to fly with them to Barcelona, spend a few days there, and then travel down the country - visiting a couple more places on-route - to spend a week at their house. Prior to Katharine's illness it had been much anticipated and looked forward to. Now it loomed scarily in front of us. We had no idea whether we should go. I suggested to Gareth that he go with William and his parents and I would stay at home with Katharine. Gareth refused to leave us. Katharine was really poorly and we were really scared for her health at this point. We were concerned that she was close to needing hospitalisation. Although she seemed strong in many ways, she looked fragile and was always cold as her body struggled to survive despite being starved.

My next suggestion was for Gareth's parents to take William on their own - I was very conscious that William really needed this holiday, as he was suffering as much as the rest of us in this tense situation - but Gareth's parents weren't confident about doing the travelling on their own. Because William and the grandparents were involved, cancelling the holiday seemed inappropriate. So we kept asking our team what to do. And we kept waiting for the next weight measurement to try and make a judgement. I guess nobody really wanted to take responsibility for the decision, including ourselves. Eventually the team suggested we go and see our GP. On the Wednesday before the Friday we were supposed to fly, Gareth, Katharine and I sat in our GP's office. He looked at us and said, "Look at you, you all look exhausted; you need a break, go and enjoy yourselves." I guess it was a relief that someone else had told us what to do. Responsibility was feeling like a huge burden.

THE REALITY

We arrived in Barcelona late in the evening. My primary concern was to check out where we could find something that Katharine would eat for breakfast. Barcelona is an amazing city and it was good to be doing something that wasn't revolving completely around anorexia. However, I was constantly scanning restaurant menus so that I knew where we might find somewhere with acceptable food. It was never about the ambience, always about the menu. We needed to stop regularly to make sure she at least had a drink. When we did stop to eat - and we had gone through the agony of her deciding what she could have - I would order her second choice for myself, so that if what she'd chosen didn't measure up, then at least we would have an alternate meal that she might eat. We left many restaurants with worried waiters or owners, as we went out looking fairly miserable with at least one meal unfinished. It was very tense, made much worse by having an extra pair of adults watching and worrying. I didn't want other people watching her. I felt they were judging both her and me. It was difficult enough for the four of us; having the children's grandparents in the mix made it even worse. They were well meaning and caring, but confused and lacking understanding.

I had reason to look at the photographs of that holiday very recently. Katharine looked absolutely awful – so ill. As I now understand is common, Katharine had developed other obsessive tendencies. So every 20 minutes or so we had to stop for her to apply sun-cream. Her low body weight made it really difficult for her to cope with the heat and she was mostly unhappy. Every evening though, we did make time to play the "Who Are You?" game. I made sure that Katharine and I had moments when we could talk, to try and keep things ok. During this time she did actually start having more to say about who she was and what she wanted to do in the future.

We eventually made it down south to Gareth's parent's house. I chose to do a lot of the cooking and food preparation just so that Katharine could be reassured that it was all ok to eat. One evening, after Katharine had gone to bed, her grandfather let off steam and had a rant about her. Unfortunately she overheard his feelings and things have never been the same since. Even now in recovery she finds it hard to forgive him. Other people didn't understand how hard it was for her – why should they? I completely understand why she was extremely frustrating for people around her. But I felt it was my job to look after her and protect her. I wanted our daughter to recover.

At their house there was less to do and so the situation was harder in some ways. Katharine resented being there. There was a lovely pool, but even though it was baking outside the water was too cold for Katharine to spend any amount of time in. She was either too cold from the water or far too hot outside. Although we had a couple of nice day trips, I think for Katharine and myself it was a relief when it was time to come home. We had seen some great things but the photos show us all looking, but not smiling a great deal. A stark contrast to the holiday of a year earlier!

Chapter 4

Rhythm, Milkshakes, Recovery

"Another page turns on the calendar, April now, not March.
....
I am spinning the silk threads of my story, weaving the
fabric of my world...I spun out of control. Eating was hard.
Breathing was hard. Living was hardest.
I wanted to swallow the bitter seeds of
forgetfulness...Somehow, I dragged myself out of the dark
and asked for help.

I spin and weave and knit my words and visions until a life
starts to take shape.

There is no magic cure, no making it all go away forever.
There are only small steps upward; an easier day, an
unexpected laugh, a mirror that doesn't matter anymore.
I am thawing."

Laurie Halse Anderson, Wintergirls

Ruth Steggles

TIME IS SLOW (AUGUST 2010 – FEBRUARY 2012)

I find the next period of time difficult even to think about, let alone write about. It was long, slow, miserable and tedious. We were surviving. We pretended with some people that we were getting by ok and others we just avoided. We kept ourselves to ourselves, it was easier that way.

THE FAMILY DYNAMIC

Several people have asked me what was going on for Gareth and William during this time. My honest answer now is I don't really know. I fed everyone and made sure they went wherever they needed to go, but personally I was so absorbed in what was going on for Katharine, I had little left to worry about the other two. I asked Gareth to share some of what he remembers:

It's hard to believe, now, that just over four years ago we were in the middle of the worst crisis that we had ever faced as a family. Our daughter, Katharine, was turning into a skeleton in front of our eyes. At one point she came within days of being admitted to hospital. We didn't know if she would even survive, let alone make a full recovery. Now, it's a bit like trying to recall a particularly horrible dream. It seems unreal, barely possible that it actually happened at all. Or maybe it's just my memory being selective, trying to protect me by blotting out the worse bits.

What I do remember though, if I really try, is…

Longing for everything to be back to normal. Desperately wanting to do something to change the situation and to help Katharine, but not knowing what, and feeling completely impotent as a consequence.

Lying in bed at night, trying to sleep, trying NOT to think about what the outcome might be. Aware that once my thoughts had started out on that route they'd be stuck on a downward spiral.

Playing the self-blame-game; what had we done wrong, what had we said or not said that precipitated this? And if it wasn't our actions, then it must have been the fault of our genes. It's got to be either Nature or

Nurture, right?

Dreading mealtimes, which had become a miserable daily battle, where they had once been a fun family time. Struggling to not nag Katharine about food or get cross with her, and often failing, badly.

Feeling incredibly sad that all of our family were suffering. Worrying how it was affecting our son, William. How it might affect our marriage if the worst happened. How it would affect Katharine's long-term health if the worst didn't happen.

WEIGHING

Each week Katharine would be weighed by one of the nurses on his way to work. This was like a pivot point in our routine. The night before being weighed would be stressful as she pondered on the potential results. She hated the experience and there was usually some fall-out of some sort; either she was disappointed (occasionally) because she hadn't put on weight and it would be longer before she could get back to exercise or, she was frightened because she had put on weight. We would often have long chats to reassure her the night before and then, after she had calmed down from her black mood as a result of the weighing, I would try and get her to talk about her feelings, again reassuring her when I could. Each week I carefully noted her weight and plotted it on a graph that I kept. On it were the weight targets for when she could return to gymnastics again and when she could start running again.

OUR SUPPORT

Katharine continued to have a regular session with her nurse, which I believe she did find useful. It was helpful that the nurse was young, fit and attractive; it made her an ideal role model for Katharine, someone who's opinion Katharine cared about and someone she could trust, at least in the beginning. Much later on, towards the second Summer of Katharine's illness, Katharine discovered me talking to her nurse about various things to do with her diet. This caused Katharine to have a fairly major strop and destroyed the trust that she had, putting a strain on their relationship from then on.

I continued to have an hour every week with another nurse, during the whole time that Katharine was being supervised by CIT. Bill would come and sit and listen to me telling him all my concerns. Just being able to voice my feelings was reassuring. Meanwhile the plan was to get Katharine to eat enough to reach a weight that the doctor in charge of her case deemed appropriate for her age and height.

FOOD AND EXERCISE

There was pressure from the wider CIT team to remove all exercise but I felt that Katharine's nurse and mine both understood the head space it gave her. Although we drastically reduced everything she was allowed to do, we agreed that she still needed to be allowed to walk for her mental well-being. I often tried to accompany her, which enabled me to moderate the pace and also talk to her, but she was also allowed to walk alone. We used exercise as a reward system and, as she re-gained weight, she was allowed to add different things back into her routines.

To begin with, Katharine drank Ensure regularly. It was reassuring for her, in that she knew what she was having and it allowed her to achieve her goals in a measured way. After a period of time, however, they were reduced and she substituted other snacks instead.

SLOW PROGRESS

That Autumn we began to see some slow progress. Her weight chart showed a steady increase from the middle of September through to March of the following year. The second half of this book goes into the details of what we were doing to support her, but briefly: We had separated Katharine and the anorexia when we spoke to her. We were playing the "Who Are You?" game regularly. As a family we had created vision boards. Katharine and I were talking much more, particularly about the future. We talked a lot about what she wanted to do and how she could achieve it. Katharine had a Reiki session quite early on. One of my friends saw her just before and just after and said it made her positively glow. Unfortunately, the practitioner that we used was quite some way from where we lived, as I think I would have used her again had she been closer. I was encouraging Katharine to listen to some guided meditations to try and help her relax. We tried to watch as many funny movies as possible as a family and I encouraged Katharine to find things to be grateful for. I also tried to encourage her to write about some of her feelings, but I don't believe she ever did. The underlying key to all this was giving her reasons to get better - things to look forward to, friendships; things she wanted to do - as well as noticing any good things we could and trying to find things that made us all feel better, here and now – walking and laughing where possible.

A DIP

In March, the steady progress we had seen over the previous six months went into reverse. I think it was just all too scary for Katharine. I think she was unsure about her ability to stop gaining weight and she didn't want to just carry on getting heavier for ever! It was just over a month after she had started running a little bit again. She no longer had that particular target weight to work towards and I think everything felt out of control for her. She also didn't really believe that her perception of what she looked like wasn't real. She has recently described to me how infuriating it was when we refused to see her and the anorexia as the same person. She didn't see the distinction, they were both her. Obviously her thoughts were her and she couldn't see the distortion in what she was thinking or seeing. It was very hard for all of us to see this decline again. We worried once more that this situation could go on for years, or for ever. Katharine lost confidence and trust. Looking back, I think perhaps she just need to spend some time coming to terms with potential recovery.

A few months later, I was invited along to a support group for parents with anorexic children. Each parent described virtually identical characteristics of their perfect child before the anorexia struck; well behaved, pleasant and high achieving. Each of us had given up something in order to help support our children. For some it was work and for others it was social or personal time. Many of the parents had children much more poorly than Katharine now was. A very brave young girl, who had fully recovered, came along with her family to talk to us. I found the whole thing pretty depressing, but the key thing for me was seeing what a long way off Katharine was from complete recovery.

ANOTHER GRIM HOLIDAY

That Summer, William had the opportunity to spend some time with his cousin in Devon, so we dropped him off and took Katharine camping in Cornwall. It was grim in many ways. At least at home we were in routine, being away brought up all the regular meal issues and just reminded us of the situation that we were in.

PELVIC SCAN AND ON THE UP AGAIN

Katharine had been having regular blood tests throughout her supervision with CIT and in the Autumn of 2011 she was also sent for a pelvic scan, to see where she was developmentally. I don't know if it was the fear of long term damage to her body, or just that she was ready to start recovering, but she once again started to regain weight.

That November we had a family photo shoot on the beach. It was great fun and it felt like Katharine had really turned a corner. Just the fact that she was happy to have her photograph taken again was a good sign!

Ruth Steggles

Chapter 5

The End of the Journey? Is This It?

"I try to be grateful for the abundance of the blessings that I have, for the journey that I'm on and to relish each day as a gift."

James McGreevey

Ruth Steggles

2012 ANOTHER YEAR

By February 2012, Katharine wasn't having much time with a nurse. The one whom she had loved and then fallen out with had gone on maternity leave; she hadn't really built up a relationship with anybody else. She was gaining weight satisfactorily and although she was a little bit off her target weight the only thing that the team were really doing was talking to me and weighing Katharine. It was decided that it was time for the CIT team to hand back to our GP. I am not sure if it was as much of a milestone for Kathrine as it was for me. I was very emotional about it and slightly scared. I felt like I had had the support I needed on tap. I understood that there were other children in more need, but it felt hard to let go. Particularly of the wonderful nurse who had supported me so well through the last 18 months. It was an amazing milestone for Katharine. She had gained enough weight to be safe. She had achieved so much to get to that point of recovery.

SO WAS SHE FULLY BETTER?

This was a partial end. It was the end of Katharine being critically ill with anorexia. She was now out of any immediate danger, but she still wasn't 100%. She laughed occasionally; I had noticed that at Christmas (an odd thing to be worthy of note!).

She was much, much better than she had been for two years. Food was still a bit tedious. There was still a certain amount of "will Katharine eat that?" She still needed her confidence boosted regularly, in particular with regard to food and body image.

We continued to talk about the future, to make plans, to notice what we have to be grateful for. To walk regularly and appreciate our natural surroundings. We planned a walking holiday for the Summer of 2012, walking round Mount Blanc, through France, Italy and Switzerland. We had to do a fair amount of training and it was good to see everyone out enjoying themselves. We became more confident in Katharine's recovery and that she really was well and leaving the anorexia behind. We had got into habits of coping with her eating "healthy food".

A WONDERFUL HOLIDAY AT LAST

We were all very excited about the holiday, travelling to Paris and taking an over-night train down to the Alps. It was raining as we got off the train, and we were all tired from travelling. We went to find somewhere for breakfast, and the obvious solution was hot chocolate and croissants – we were in France! Everything had led us to believe that it would be ok and she would cope. I think being over tired contributed to make it a disaster. Katharine refused to eat on the morning we had planned to start a 10 mile walk with several thousand feet of ascent. We were all so cross, upset and frankly scared. Katharine stormed off somewhere leaving the three of us to contemplate our breakfast, weary and shell shocked.

At last I found her and took her to a super market. Where I explained quite clearly that unless she ate we weren't walking anywhere. Eventually we all calmed down and Katharine found something she wanted to eat. There was one more food incident during the holiday. We were staying in refuges (similar to youth hostels, but food is provided) and one night the menu included chips. Not something we have ever particularly eaten as a family and certainly not since Katharine had been ill. She had the sense to take me aside and just explain that it was a bit scary. I reassured her but she still wasn't comfortable eating them. She happily ate seconds of the stew that they came with and for the sake of the holiday we just let it drop. At that time I still didn't know if this was always going to echo in the back ground.

As with the Spanish trip there were more suntan lotion stops than would be normal, but relatively speaking it was so much better than before it hardly seemed worth commenting on. So with not much more than the usual holiday trauma, a day of rain in the mountains, a stolen camera, sore feet and broken walking boots we had an amazing holiday. I guess that we had reached a level that we could cope with.

WHAT NOW?

It is funny how, looking back now, each time I do look back I see more progress. When you are in a situation it is hard to see what is going on. My husband has done a photo book for our son this year as he turned 18. I was shocked at how awful Katharine looked in the summer of 2010. Even though at the time I knew she looked awful, I think I protected myself from the true horror of it.

This Summer, Katharine has been out without any suntan lotion on! She tells me in front of her friends that when she is out with them she has had pizza. She eats lots, although nothing processed particularly, but I don't feel that is something she needs to change.

Katharine has seen an endocrinologist and there seems to be no lasting damage to her body. She has worked very hard this year and taken her GCSEs. Dressing for Prom was very traumatic for both of us. She still doesn't like the way she looks, and lacks confidence on such occasions. It would be easy to lump this with anorexia, but I also think that there is a lot of pressure on being a teenager these days and I know for certain that many of her friends have similar anxiety over similar things. I see her growing in confidence and learning more about herself as time goes by.

As I write this, Katharine is away on a school-run expedition to Malawi. She was very apprehensive about going. Her worries were largely about being sick away from home. I had to sign a medical declaration form and disclose any potential risks or previous illness that could cause problems while they were away for a month in Africa. I thought really long and hard about this. I think that she has been through some stuff, and learnt a lot. She still has things to learn about herself, her diet, and other people. She has fears, worries and she lacks confidence sometimes. She has more tools than she used to, but I don't believe she still suffers from anorexia. I didn't declare anything on her medical form. I am certain she will have a great time and whatever happens she will come back having learnt some more.

HER PERMISSION

When someone first suggested to me that I should be working with children and families of children with anorexia, my first though was that I wanted Katharine to be comfortable with it. She still had moments of guilt (for which I think there is no need) about what she put everyone else through. So it is with her support that I started this project. Like me, I think that she would like as much good as possible to come out of this whole process. Writing this together has been part of our journey to learning and understanding more.

LOOK FOR THE GIFT

Believe me when I say that I have felt a pain that is likely to be similar to yours. I felt desperate, and times felt dark. However we have all learnt a lot. We were presented with this massive challenge, and when it was with us we had no idea if or how we would get through it. But we have; Katharine has shown incredible strength and is learning about the benefits of vulnerability. Gareth and William showed immense patience, caring and consideration. I suspect we are all stronger for having been there and I am certain that both Katharine and I have learnt a huge amount about ourselves and each other.

AND FINALLY.....

The other day we went out for a meal as a family. It was to a very nice restaurant. We had all dressed up and we were celebrating Katharine finishing her GCSEs and William getting a place at college. The place was great, the food delicious and we all had a really lovely time. It brings tears to my eyes now just thinking about it! We used to love going out for meals and we can do it again now and it is all alright. We have two amazing children and we have learnt a lot. They both had a really rough time, as did Gareth and I, but we survived and you can too!

Part 2

Helping Your Child Recover

Ruth Steggles

INTRODUCTION

I believe this is a process in which you need to acknowledge where you are, understand something about the problem, look at how that might be addressed and then go round again. As with much learning, this spirals each time you revisit something you understand a bit more. In this section I take you through the techniques I used in the order in which they are immediately applicable. You do not have to have read the whole of Part Two to use what I have told you. This is a relatively quick read so you may want to get a complete overview by reading the whole lot. If you choose to do that I would encourage you to then come back and work through this second part chapter by chapter. It is intentionally written in a way that means you can read Chapter Six and then take action from it straight away.

Each chapter builds on the one before and will enhance your understanding as you go. Revisit sections regularly, work at a pace that suits you, but do actually try some of the things I suggest. Reading the book won't solve the problem, but putting into action some of the ideas I talk about will certainly help. Approach everything I say with an open mind, try the things I suggest with an open heart. Many of the things I talk about are incredibly simple; I often see people overlooking the simplest things in life because they see them as of no value. I would argue that many of these simple things are the most valuable. Please try, experiment, take notes and try again. Find what works for you and your unique family and circumstances, but don't give up on the first attempt; perseverance is key here.

SETTING THE SCENE

It may surprise you to know that this isn't all about your child. There are parts of this book that are about you. I need to say here that there is no blame and it is not your fault (I will expand on this in a moment) but if you are in a better place it will massively help your child. When our children are young it can be relatively easy to give them instructions and tell them what to do. As they get older and believe themselves to be more competent, we mostly have to lead by example, so often in the book I will encourage you to do things before expecting your child to follow.

JOURNALING

Journaling is an incredibly useful process. It is a posh word for writing. Some key things about it are:

- It is writing just for you no one else needs to ever see this.
- Don't think too hard, just write what comes.
- What you write may or may not be your truth, but writing it may help you to see that.
- Don't stop yourself writing anything that comes to you; there is no right or wrong here.
- Don't judge what you write in any way.

Many people can't process things effectively in their head. Writing something down brings it out of your head and can lead to a number of things from nothing to relief, acknowledgement or clarity. Sometimes I write something and notice that I used to think or feel that way, but writing it has helped me to let it go of it. I would encourage you from now on to keep a note book to jot down anything that comes to you, any questions you want answered, anything you are noticing or feeling. Have it by you as you read this book, look at it and write in it regularly. Over time you will see progress that might, without this kind of record, go unnoticed.

BREATHING

I suspect that if you are like me you are keen to get into the content of this book but I want to take a moment to draw your attention to this incredible tool that we carry with us 24/7. I talk to clients a lot about their breath; we have all been breathing quite successfully since we were born, but often we don't recognise that. Awareness of our breath and how we are breathing can be used as a really effective tool. When people get stressed or angry their breathing tends to get fast and/or shallow. Learning to be aware of these changes allows us to change how we breathe and as a result to change how we feel. Deep breathing is a way in which we can practice becoming aware.

When I work with clients, we nearly always start by taking three deep breaths. This changes how we feel, it changes how we hold our bodies and enables us to relax a little. You are potentially going through a worrying and stressful time; consciously using your breath will create some space for you which will help you cope.

DEEP BREATHING

Use this when you notice that you are feeling stressed, when you are over-worrying or when something has been said that pushes your buttons, or if you are about to do or say something that you know you need to be calm for. Use this often whenever you think it will help you.

Stop for a moment, take a really deep breath, and notice your lungs really stretching out as far as they can. Hold your breath for a couple of seconds and then let it all out, emptying every last bit of breath. Pause for a moment and repeat this twice more.

I'd like you to try this now, but before you do, just quickly check in with your body, how are you feeling; are you tense? What is going on in your head? What pictures are you seeing in your mind? Do the exercise, then just check out to see if any of the things you noticed before have changed.

When you are in the heat of the moment it is not necessary to do the checking out before and after; just notice that you are getting stressed, stop and take three deep breaths, pausing with full lungs, and then again with empty ones. If you find yourself getting stressed or frustrated, with life yourself or anorexia, just remember your breath and take a moment to breathe deeply. It will give you some time and space and help you to respond rather than react.

In Chapter Nine, as well as some meditation techniques, I will teach you a breathing exercise for deep relaxation that will benefit anyone who chooses to do it.

BEING OUT IN NATURE AND WALKING

I also cover this in detail in Chapter Nine but I believe it is significant enough that I draw your attention to it as part of setting the scene for the work there is to do. Much of the time when Katharine was ill felt very stressful. We were anxious, cross and worried. The waiting rooms and consulting rooms were often hot and oppressive. Stopping in a park or walking in the fields and hills behind our house had a significant positive affect on our mood, how we thought, and how felt. We found it far easier to communicate outside than inside. I can understand that getting outside may not feel like an important enough thing to do when everything else seems to be falling apart, but trust me when I say it will support everyone, and from now on try to get into nature as often as you can.

ACTION POINTS

At the end of each chapter I have given you some action points so that you can actually start doing something other than just reading. It is the action that will make the change, not just reading the book. Whilst this book is primarily designed for parents or carers, it is possible that someone suffering with anorexia might also read it. I have given action points that they might choose to do at the end of the chapters too. These are designed for them to do if they choose, not for you to enforce and tell them to do. If you simply do the things I suggest for you, you will achieve the outcomes you want.

Chapter 6

I Blame the Parents

"Discontent, blaming, complaining, self-pity cannot serve as a foundation for a good future, no matter how much effort you make."

Eckhart Tolle

Ruth Steggles

IT IS NOT YOUR FAULT BUT IT IS YOUR PROBLEM.

I remember, before Katharine was ill, the mother of one of her friends saying about anorexia, "I blame the parents!" At the time I thought nothing of it but later these words came back to haunt me. They played round and round in my head tormenting me, whispering to me, gently stroking the guilt that was ripe to grow. I regularly asked myself "what had we done wrong?", or more specifically "what had I done wrong?" I presumed if one person felt it was my fault then others would too.

WHAT THIS CHAPTER IS ALL ABOUT

In this chapter I want to give you absolute reassurance that it is not your fault, and help you understand what you need to have, be and think to make a difference to your child. This chapter is about "mind-set." If you are committed to help your child, your mind-set is key. We explore where you are now and what you are feeling, in order that you can use that to support you in the task that lies ahead. (I needed to acknowledge the situation we were in before I could start to find ways in which to improve it.) We explore the emotional roller coaster you might be experiencing and look at how you might turn that into a positive force for change. I encourage you to recognise the resources you have to give you the courage you need to help your child.

IT IS NOT YOUR FAULT OR THEIRS, BUT IT IS YOUR PROBLEM

Have you found yourself searching for what went wrong, where this could have come from, where it started? Was it things you said or did, the people your child mixes with, the magazines they read? You need to understand it is no body's fault.

The fact that it wasn't anybody's fault was the most useful thing I read in any of the text-book like books I had been able to track down on eating disorders. Janet Treasure's words from her book anorexia nervosa – a survival guide for families, friends and sufferers gave me some relief: "The illness often arises out of a complex mixture of many factors. It is easier to draw up a list of what anorexia nervosa is not rather than suggest what it is:

- "It is not an indication that parents have gone badly wrong bringing up their child.
- "It is not a phase of silly, stubborn naughtiness.
- "Nor is it something that sufferers can "Just snap out of"."

I think there is still a feeling among the general public that people bring it upon themselves, possibly due to inappropriate messages in the media. Nothing could be further from the truth. In our case I could see any number of potential contributory factors, not least Katharine's personality trait of always striving for success, but ultimately it is a whole mixture of genetics and circumstance that lead to anorexia. For many people it is a mixture of things coming together.

No one deliberately creates this fear and anxiety in their life.Most importantly trying to apportion blame to anyone or anything is of no help in terms of moving forward and recovering.

ACKNOWLEDGE DON'T BLAME
It is vital to accept that it is no-one's fault because until you do it will be much harder to deal with the situation that needs to be confronted. If you blame your child for the situation you are all in, you will find it much harder to help them. If you blame yourself, your guilt will prevent you from finding the strength you need to help tackle what lies ahead.

The purpose of this book is to support recovery and a search for blame in my view is a waste of precious energy. A great start for you is to make the assumption that it is no one's fault. Next is to accept where you are.

Once you have accepted that it is no-one's fault, you then need to recognise that even though you haven't created the situation it is still your problem. If you look only to others to solve it, the journey is going to be a much harder and longer. Accepting that you have a problem and taking ownership to help improve the situation will ultimately lead to results. I am not suggesting for one minute that you don't use all the resources around you. Work with whatever medical help you can get, use whatever resources you can find, but ultimately you know your child better than anyone else. As you start to take responsibility, begin to trust your instincts. When you spend time observing, writing and reflecting you will find that you actually know more than you thought. Without realising it, you will have very likely been spending a lot time with your child, which means that you do have more resources than you realise.

RECOGNISE YOUR EMOTIONS

It is tempting just to put how you feel aside and concentrate completely on your child; after all this illness is not your fault and it is they who are ill. However, if you are going to help them you need to get some things clear for yourself. As you learn to recognise and communicate your own feelings and emotions you are demonstrating a useful and healthy skill for your child. If you learn how to feel and still be ok, then they can too.

WRITE HOW YOU FEEL

Let us start by you acknowledging how you feel. Spend a moment noticing what you are going through; what emotions have you been experiencing over the last few months, weeks or even years? What do you really feel? What conversations are happening in your head, what pictures are you playing through your brain? I don't want you to judge this in any way; I just want you to be really honest with yourself. This isn't about blaming or criticism. It might be helpful to find a quiet place, relax for a moment, maybe sit and just notice your breath coming in and out of your nostrils. When you are ready just write whatever comes into your head about what you have been going through. You never have to show this to anyone else. Write absolutely everything that comes up.

EXPLORE WHAT YOU HAVE WRITTEN

When you have done that sit for a short while, and then you may want to read what you have written. As you look at the words on the paper, are there any that you really feel, what are you seeing? What are you telling yourself? If there are some that really stand out, take each one in turn and just allow yourself to experience that feeling. It is all ok and you are safe.

ALLOW AND DON'T JUDGE

Feelings and emotions come and go. If we experience something in one moment it doesn't have to stay that way. Often, by recognising our feelings or thoughts, we are able to let them go; it is a very healing thing to do. For some emotions, simply acknowledging them will allow them to dissipate; denying them or suppressing them is not helpful for you long term. Allow what comes up to come without judgement. Find somewhere to cry or shout if you need to, but let them out.

For me a big feeling was grief for the daughter we had lost; I was worried she could die or possibly worse, be this way forever. I was scared, worried, tense, lost and feeling alone, isolated, feeling inadequate. Some people feel embarrassed or angry. Whatever it is, it is ok. None of this is a reflection on anybody or anything else.

WHAT IF I FEEL NOTHING?

It is quite possible that you have got so used to supressing your own feelings and thoughts that it seems as if you feel nothing. Can you see anything in your mind, can you hear anything in your brain? If not, that is ok at the moment. As you start on this journey with your child I believe that over time you will allow yourself to experience more, whether it is how you feel, what you see or how you acknowledge the conversations in your head. But now it is about accepting yourself the way you are and about being kind to yourself. If you can learn to treat yourself with love and respect, you will be able to lead by example and teach your child to treat themnselves with love and respect.

HAVE I GOT WHAT IT TAKES? HOW CAN I HELP THEM WHEN THE PROFESSIONALS ARE STRUGGLING?

One of the problems with professional support is that unless your child has been taken into a specialist unit (something I knew I didn't want to happen), they are unlikely to have daily support from a trained professional. Once anorexia has taken hold, you are working with an entrenched habit. Habits are rarely broken with a one hit wonder. Even with a very effective therapy session where someone's thinking can sometimes be changed in an instant, the longevity of that change will depend on creating an environment and a strategy for breaking that habit over a period of time.

There are a few things you have over and above a specialist:
  • You know your child better than anyone else. You have spent more

years with them and watched their likes and dislikes for a long time. When you learn to trust your instincts through this book you will know what is right and wrong.

- You are around more than a professional can be.
- You care about them more than anyone else in the world does.
- Strategies and techniques can be learnt but the way you feel for your child, the knowledge you have of them and the time you spend with them are difficult for a professional to emulate.

DO YOU LOVE YOUR CHILD?

Forgive me asking, but this is very important for you to know. The emotions you have just acknowledged may make it hard to be clear about this just at the moment. The child you thought you knew may seem to have changed, they don't do as you ask; they may be isolated and uncommunicative. So it is possible that at the moment you don't like them very much. What I want you to consider is how you felt when you brought them into the world. Cast your mind back to the happy times you have had, picture them in the times when you knew without a doubt that you loved every inch of them. Look at old photographs of them, paintings they have done, words they wrote as a younger child. Really embrace that feeling, picture how it was, see it in your mind's eye, hear the laughter, feel the joy, experience that love at its deepest level (even if it makes you cry). You may want to write some of this in your journal.

SAVE THAT FEELING

Find something that reminds you of them, something that you can easily keep nearby or carry with you. It could be something small they have given you, or a shell you found on a beach together or even a hair bobble or badge they often wore. Hold it between your thumb and second finger while you picture a time when you were completely in love with them, see the colours, notice what can you hear, what you are feeling. Spend a few seconds really being in that moment. Feeling the love and the joy of it. As you feel the emotions really peak, squeeze the object you have between your thumb and finger, then just relax. Give yourself a little shake to lose that feeling and then repeat it twice more, giving yourself a shake between each.

Test the feeling: without trying to create the picture yourself, squeeze your object between your finger and thumb, what do you notice? If that doesn't recreate the emotion you may want to practise this process until just squeezing the object helps you experience those emotions of love. Don't get hung up on creating this if you find it hard to do, maybe come back and try it again another time. Trust that feeling is still in there, the love you have for your child; it is those feelings and that picture of them that are going to give you the strength to help now.

On this journey you are now embarking upon, come back regularly to this emotion, this picture. Squeeze your object between your fingers, carry it with you all the time. When times are tough and things aren't going the way you hoped. When life is fraught, frustrating and you are drawn in to arguments, remember this. Remember you love your child and trust me that you can help them come back. When you find this feeling and allow it to grow deep within you, you have the strength to do anything.

THE EMBARRASSMENT FACTOR

Whilst I was writing this book I came across the case of a young girl whose parents were so embarrassed that their daughter had anorexia they told everyone that she had leukaemia. This particular girl died just before she received her A level results. I found it really shocking that people should feel that way. It makes me realise how important it is to recognise where you are in order to be able to change the situation. You don't have to shout about it to everyone, but be honest with yourself; you have nothing to be ashamed of and nothing to be embarrassed about.

You love your child, you are in a dark place, but you can make a difference. At times like this trying to pretend that everything is ok all the time will not be helpful. You are stronger than you think and there are things you can do to really help your child. Part of the process is that you must look after yourself which I discuss in more detail in Chapter Nine. The acknowledgement you have started in this chapter is the first step in that process. You need to look after yourself and also seek support where you can get it.

YOU NEED TO START THE PROCESS

For me one of the flaws of the help we were offered was that it seem to rely on waiting till Katharine was at a safe weight* and waiting until she was ready to get better. For me, both of those things seemed too far away and much too passive.

Eventually for full recovery your child will have to take a lot of personal responsibility, but the nature of the illness is such that their complete acceptance of that responsibility in the early days is unlikely. As a parent, once we take ownership we can start on the road to recovery. And here is the bitter sweet truth (that may put you off what I have to say for ever). This whole situation may be a gift in disguise when you come through this if you decide to play your part and take responsibility; your relationship with your child could be better than ever before. Through this scary horrible time there is the potential for massive growth, for you, for your family relationships and for your child.

These days, when Katharine is going through some normal teenage trauma, I just point out to her what she has already achieved and overcome, how strong she has already shown herself to be. We communicate on a much deeper level than we did before her illness and we have both learnt so much. As a family we hung together through tough times and I am certain it has deepened the respect that my husband and I have for one another.

"Anorexia" is such a horrible word. It's a harsh, frequently misused and misunderstood label. For me, the word anorexia, holds connotations of clinical waiting rooms and hours spent sitting with patronising psychiatrists, it was not part of me. Anorexia is never a word I associated with myself, never a word I wanted to associate with myself, I resented the label and rebelled against anything that reinforced the fact I was "anorexic." What is anorexia? Is it an illness, a disease, a mental disorder or something we bring on ourselves, for the attention? It is a word that so many people don't understand, like the majority of mental illnesses; people who have not suffered with a similar issue cannot possibly comprehend

*how consuming and real it is. I don't even like calling it a
"mental issue," the word mental just implies that the person
is not quite right, crazy. So many people use the word
anorexia flippantly, as an insult, loaded with judgement. I
lose count of the number of times I have heard someone call
someone else anorexic purely because they are skinny or do
not eat a lot. One particular comment that sticks in my mind
is when a friend recently said, after travelling in Africa,
"You see all these starving children who have no choice and
then at home there are so many young girls who are
anorexic." I have to bite my tongue when a comment like this
is made, because I know that really I can't blame them for
not understanding, I certainly didn't before I became ill. I
always resented the label "anorexic", it was just so not me. I
was not one of those girls who went on stupid diets, who
didn't eat in front of boys, who were labelled "anorexic," I
was sensible. What people don't understand is that anorexia
is not a choice, not something we can control or do just to be
awkward. I want people to understand that "mental
illnesses" for want of a better word, are no different to other
illnesses. Just like cancer cells, it's something that grows
inside, starting small but expanding exponentially, through
no choice of our own, spreading the illness throughout the
body. A growth, or negativity, that needs to be cut out just
like cancer. It is not part of us, we do not call cancer
patients, "cancers." Anorexia is an illness that does not
belong in the body. And just like any other illness, it is a
product of circumstance, genetic tendencies, personality traits,
influences of our day to day lives. In no way should there be
any blame. Please do not blame yourself, or your child."*

CHAPTER SUMMARY

You can know that this is not your fault. It is safe to feel whatever you feel and it is good to acknowledge your emotions. You do have resources to help your child, and the opinions of other people with no experience of this are often misguided. Decide now to play your part in helping your child to find a way to help themselves. In the beginning it may be just you doing this; in time they will tentatively start to join you. Eventually they will be able to take full responsibility and grow into the independent person they were meant to be. In the next chapter I am going to suggest some techniques that you can start to explore, but for the moment take some time to do the following things.

Your job now is:
- To accept that you can help
- Work on your own emotions so that you are in a position of strength to help your child
- To decide to help your child get better
- To start learning to believe you can make a difference

ACTION POINTS FOR YOU
- Take some time out to acknowledge your feelings, express them out loud somewhere safe or write them down.
- Start being kind to yourself and recognising, how much you love your child.
- Decide you are going to make a difference.
- Start asking questions; what do you want to know? Write these down, think about who might be the person to give the answers or where might you find them.

ACTION FOR YOUR CHILD:
- If you have read this chapter you might want to write or draw about what it makes you feel.

*Safe Weight –the medical profession have charts that indicate the average weight of the population and what constitutes a healthy weight for a given age and height.

Ruth Steggles

Chapter 7

Understanding Anorexia

"Happy are those who dare courageously to defend what they love."

Ovid

Ruth Steggles

YOUR CHILD AND THE ANOREXIA ARE NOT THE SAME.

The person sitting at our dinner table scared and lying to us was not the gorgeous daughter we knew. Katharine didn't lie, she was confident and caring, but the young girl now in her place was not just physically smaller, shrivelled and grey; her personality had changed, the words that came out of her mouth seemed to bear no relationship to reality. I occasionally saw glimpses of the girl we had lost; after fights and tears she would some-times come and apologise. What was going on, where was she?

WHAT THIS CHAPTER IS ALL ABOUT

In this chapter I help you to notice that you have a voice in your own head that is separate from who you are, in order to help you to understand what is happening for your child. I explain the anorexic bully and help you to separate the anorexia from your child. This will help your child eventually to separate themselves from the anorexia. I suggest ways in which you can manage your conversations in order to have more effective communication. Finally I help you to manage your expectations about the recovery process.

THE VOICE IN *YOUR* HEAD

Have you ever listened to the voice in your head, you know the one that tells you what you should or shouldn't do? You probably have several. If you actually stop and listen you may notice that your mind has a constant stream of noise going on. A commentary of what you should and shouldn't be doing. We are sometimes able to choose what we listen to and what we want to do; however we do often believe that what we think is the truth. It is helpful to understand that those thoughts are all judgement and not fact; they are all a running dialogue of our brain's interpretation of what is going on. The truth is that we do believe the majority of what we tune into. So unless you have spent some time in this state of awareness you are likely to go along with what your brain tells you.

THOUGHTS IN THE NIGHT

Have you ever woken up in the night with something on your mind and in your dopey state gone over and over it unable to sleep? Looking at things from different angles, thoughts rolling over and over in your mind not making any real sense. In the middle of the night it all seems pretty major. If you have, then you have had experience of obsessive and exaggerated thoughts to a small degree at least. Let us also bear in mind that when we are awake we tend to assume that what our brain tells is fact!

BRAIN PLASTICITY

What is great about the brain is that the way it functions and processes is not fixed indefinitely. Scientific research these days is very clear that we can change connections in the brain and alter the way in which we perceive things. The book Mom Please Help spends some considerable time explaining the brain's ability to make new pathways and as a result act differently (neuro plasticity). The ideas that I talk about in this book are all designed to help support these changes in the process of your child's recovery. In learning about this and supporting your child to change, your own thinking and awareness will also develop and grow.

START NOTICING YOUR OWN INTERNAL VOICE

As you go about your daily life, noticing your own internal voice can be really helpful. When something happens one or more of our senses observe it. Our brain then receives the information and the thing we often forget or don't notice is that our brain then interprets what has been observed. This is crucial, because it is this interpretation that determines how we then react or respond to whatever happens. That interpretation is based on our beliefs and the constant internal conversations we have with ourselves.

For example: You are walking down the street and notice your neighbour so you say hello. He just walks on. You are suddenly really cross and thinking, "what a rude man!" There may have been many explanations; he may simply not have heard or seen you, he may have had some really bad news that morning and been completely preoccupied, he may have been embarrassed because he didn't recognise you, or he may have assumed you were taking to someone else. However, the way you responded was all down to your own internal interpretation, not the facts of the situation.

Most people assume that when something happens it is the event happening that determines the outcome.

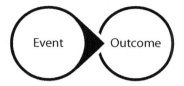

In reality, when an event happens we interpret what that means and it is this interpretation that creates the outcome.

"We see the world, not as it is, but as we are—or, as we are conditioned to see it."
Stephen R. Covey, The 7 Habits of Highly Effective People: Powerful Lessons in Personal Change

When we have high self-esteem and awareness (feel good about ourselves), our internal conversations tend to be much healthier than when we have low self-esteem or self-awareness.

AN ANOREXIC BRAIN
In your child's brain, two things have happened:

1. Their brain has fallen into an obsessive pattern of fear and anxiety. One of the ways this comes out is in the form of the stories they have created about food, what, how much, when they can eat etc. as a result of internal conversations they have had with themselves. Their relationship with food is a symptom and what may currently be making them unhealthy, but this is a symptom, not the cause.

2.   Their low body weight has exacerbated this by impairing brain function. So the story line that their brain is telling has become

massively distorted. In a similar way to us, they think that their brain is telling them the truth, and like us they think their brain is behaving rationally so no amount of persuading is going to convince them otherwise. Just telling them they are wrong is not going to make any difference.

Your child is likely to be very scared, and certainly very anxious. They are likely to believe most of the time that that they have to behave the way they do in order to survive, to be worthy, in order to have friends or any number of other things they think they need. It is very hard for them to trust anything outside the conversation in their head because this internal conversation is very real to them and a lot of the things they may be hearing from you disagree with what their head is telling them. (Do you remember the last time your partner told you that you were wrong over something? Did you immediately accept what they were saying and agree cordially and say of course yes you are right darling? I know that is not what happens to me. I immediately look to justify my position and confirm why I know I am right).

THE ANOREXIC BULLY
Separating the anorexia and your Child
Understanding your child and anorexia as separate is immensely helpful. In the same way that you are not your thoughts and neither are they. Yes they are being bullied and yes the anorexia seems to be taking over and is a huge part of who is currently getting the upper hand in how they are behaving, but the anorexia is absolutely not your child!!!! Inside, behind that bullying voice your child is still there with all the wonderful qualities that you used to love about them. Your job with the help of the people around you is to help this side of them emerge once more, so that they can once again hear their own internal voice clearly over the racket of the anorexia. Understanding that your child and the anorexia are different is one of the keys to effective communication that will enable you to help them. The language you use from now on needs to make this distinction and in doing so you will help them dissociate from the anorexia.

Your child may or may not be able to make this distinction at the moment. In her book Mealtimes and Milestones, Constance Barter gives a very clear picture of what it was like for her, how she could hear the anorexic voice in her head and how persuasive it was as it told her it had befriended her when everyone else had abandoned her. Her description shows how in the beginning the anorexia had majority hold of internal conversations, but as time goes on Constance's own desire for a life free of this pain and heartache allows her to hear a healthier internal dialogue.

"If you are reading this book because your child or someone close to you is suffering with anorexia, the most important message I would like you to be able to take is to separate your child and the "anorexia." They are not doing it out of spite, I knew whilst I was ill the amount of pain I was putting my family through, I felt I had no choice and I absolutely despised myself for it. Of course I blamed myself and I know it was hard for my family not to blame me, how could they understand? At the same time I know my parents carried a whole lot of blame themselves."

IT IS OK TO DISLIKE THE ANOREXIA

It is ok, in fact it is helpful to not like the anorexia. I think it is ok to have negative emotions towards the anorexia, but it is not ok for these to be directed at your child. You are in really trying times, and however much you try to stay calm, understand the situation, be resourceful and patient there are times when you will just be exceptionally frustrated. Most people are likely to get pretty cross on occasion; you are after all human. At times like this being exasperated with the anorexia is so much healthier than being exasperated with your child. I know in the heat of the moment it is easy to lose sight of the difference, but if you can possibly make the distinction, it preserves your relationship with your child in a much healthier manner. It is likely that in the moments that your child is able to experience themselves they already have a feeling of guilt. Blaming them, which is what your frustration is likely to sound like, is not going to help in any way. It really is ok to start expressing some emotion but care is needed with the words you use and how it is expressed. By separating the anorexia and your child in your own head you are able to talk about why you want them to be better. How much you love them and how you can see that the anorexia isn't helping (they are very likely to believe it is helping them and believe it more than they believe you in the beginning).

"During my illness there was a constant cycle of fights and apologies. An argument of some sort would occur during every meal time, fuelling this stupid voice in my head, causing it to rebel further. These were the moments where I was not myself; there is no space for logical thought. Yet in the heat of the moment, it feels like yourself, it's in your head, how can it possibly be separate? In the moments of calm, logical thought would creep in and I would be overwhelmed with guilt, what a stupid situation. This illness literally took over my every thought, a constant battle of guilt and angst. It was exhausting and depressing; there was nothing else in my life."

CHANGING YOUR CONVERSATION
Notice first

Even before you start changing the language you use, start observing what is going on for your child. Can you ever catch them being themselves, the lovely child who used to be a joy to have around? A momentary glimpse can make you feel so much better, so just be aware and notice when you see them. You may want to write what you notice in your journal. It may be far easier to see and hear the anorexia. You are likely to recognise the voice immediately, it is likely to have been prevalent lately. It might be about body image, what they can and can't eat, or simply denial that anything is wrong. Spending some time distinguishing before you say anything can be really helpful. If you can't at this moment in time see or hear your child as you used to know them, don't panic, they are in there and you really can help to get them back. Spend some time thinking about how you want to introduce the idea of talking to the anorexia separately before you mention it to your child.

Comment on desired behaviour

If you are really lucky, it may be that there are times that your child really is the person you used to know. If you see moments like this and they are doing something or behaving in a way that you can complement them on without being patronising, do so. Give a specific compliment about their behaviour. "It was really thoughtful the way you decided to do that for Grandma, thank you." Or "You are a really thoughtful friend, it was nice that you called Sarah today when you knew she was feeling blue." I would avoid it if it is to do with food. One of the behaviours we saw in Katharine was that in the early days she became obsessed with creating and preparing food for others, something they want to be involved in but then deny themselves.

Some conversation openers....

Would it be ok for us to have a chat later? Is there anywhere you would like to go?

How are you feeling?

What is going on for you at the moment?

What worries you most at the moment?

You seem sad, is that about anything in particular?

You were obviously cross with me earlier, I am not sure exactly what upset you, can you help me understand?

PLAN IMPORTANT CONVERSATIONS

All the above are just suggestions and spending some time thinking about things you genuinely want to know is helpful. If you can start to understand how they are feeling and notice their language, then over time you can start to understand what is important to them, what scares them, and find ways to support and reassure them around those fears. If you are able to talk back to them using their language about their fears when it is your turn to talk they will hear you better. I wrote lots of notes I would think about questions that I thought may help in advance, sometimes I used them and sometimes I didn't, but having thought about the conversation beforehand helped me really be with Katharine and listen.

DON'T BE FRIGHTENED OF SILENCE

Your child may have nothing to say and no answers. Don't fill the space with gabble; time sitting together saying nothing is still connecting. Give them space and plenty of time to think and answer. Even if they are saying nothing, the fact that you took the time to ask will be important to them. Simply asking the questions will allow them to sit and think about the answers they may genuinely not know, but thinking about how they are feeling and what is going on for them over a period of time is helpful. When your child has had a lot of time and you have really listened, these are some of the things you may want to say to them:

I really care about you and very much want you to lead a healthy and fulfilling life. I can see that anorexia is sometimes controlling your actions. I love you very much and I really want to talk to you and help you, but I don't want to be nice to the anorexia because I don't believe it has got your best interests at heart. I am here for you and I am going to do everything I can to help you live the life you want. From now on I am going to listen and talk to you but not the anorexia.

When you are in conversation, be aware of who is speaking. If you are hearing the anorexia moaning or laying the law down at the dinner table then make it very clear that you don't wish to talk to anorexia, it has no place at the table. This is the kind of thing that happened to us: "That sounds like anorexia talking, if you have something to say Katharine we would love to hear it but I don't want to talk to anorexia." At other times you might hear your child. Sometimes Katharine would outright say that she was scared or apologise for behaving in a certain way. When she was scared I would listen and reassure her that she was doing a great job and that she would get to a place where she wasn't scared and it would be alright. When she apologised I would empathise that I knew how hard it was not to allow the anorexia bully to make her behave in certain ways, that I knew it was the anorexia and not her. If it felt appropriate I would sometimes go on to ask her what happened and see if she had any ideas as to how she could act differently if the same thing happened again.

PLANNING CONVERSATIONS

Important conversations need planning and preparation. They don't work in a hurry or in the heat of the moment. There is a process you need to plan in order to maximise your chance of achieving what you want. S O S L S L A

Space	Where and when would be a good time to have this conversation?
Outcome	Why do you want this conversation and what do you hope to achieve from it?
Sate	How are you feeling emotionally? What state are you in?
Listen	It is really important to create time to really listen to your child.
State	Say what you need to say.
Listen	Make space to listen again.
Agree or (conclude)	Agree on an outcome (when they are very ill you may have to conclude).

SPACE – CREATING IT

Where and when would be a good place to talk? It is important to have critical conversations away from the dining table. At food times the chances of your child being tense are very high. Where would be a good space for you? It sounds slightly trivial but mutual territory can be helpful. Their bedroom or your office/kitchen may cause conflict simply by an underlying recognition about who is in charge in this space. We had three places that really worked for us. Katharine had a small snug that was comfortable, calm and non-threatening; it was her space, somewhere she felt comfortable, but not the same as me invading her bedroom. In the car was often handy for on-going discussions. Because of where we live, I do quite a lot of taxi driving for our children. Sitting beside one another not facing is a non-confrontational way to talk about things. Both the down side and the upside of this are that you are both stuck there for a period of time. The other downside is that when you are driving, you are not giving the other person 100% of your attention, so this is better for low key conversations than really critical ones. Finally and most effective for us was that we walked a lot outside. Not fast exercise walking but slow gentle strolls outside in lovely places. Again I will talk more about this in Chapter Nine.

There is something very helpful about being alongside one another either sitting or walking. Facing someone can be perceived as aggressive or threatening. If you are facing a problem it sits between you. When you are side by side the problem is in front of you both, so you can face it together. It can create a less threatening and more supportive way to interact.

OUTCOMES

Why do you want to have a conversation with your child, what do you want the outcome to be? What is the most important thing about having this conversation? Is it about you understanding what they are thinking or is it about something you need to communicate to them? What would you like to happen as a result of the conversation? Iis this about information or are you hoping that there will be a change in actions by either you, your child or other people? Think through your perfect outcome, but also think about what the minimum acceptable outcome would be for you. What is the smallest change or step that you would consider to be progress? It might be as simple as creating a way in which you can both talk.

In thinking about your outcomes, if you only consider what you want and why it has to change because of your agenda then it may be tricky to communicate. Know what you really want for your child. Why do you care about them? How you would like things to turn out for them? Whenever you start a conversation with their best interests at heart, you are much more likely to communicate better. Don't let it be about venting or frustration.

STATE

Your state, how you are feeling, is really important. Make sure that you are ready emotionally to have the conversation. No matter how well chosen the words that come out of our mouth, how you are feeling will be evident to the other person. Our body, how we hold it, how we move and breathe all tell the truth about what is really going on inside. When we see other people saying one thing but their body tells us something else we distrust them even if we don't know why. It is far easier to adjust your state than try and make your body lie. The breathing exercise I mentioned at the start of Part Two of this book will help; remember the things we talked about in Chapter Six. Remember how you love your child, remember why you want them to get better for them; fill yourself with feelings and pictures of love and caring, let those emotions wash away the anger and frustration. When we communicate with an open and caring heart we connect with the other person far more effectively. In Chapter Nine we will explore more ways of managing your own state.

LISTEN

"Seek first to understand, then to be understood."
Stephen R. Covey

One of my favourite stories on this subject is from Stephen Covey, the businessman and keynote speaker, which goes something like this: "I was listening to a man one day and he was saying, "I don't understand my son he just doesn't listen to me"" I asked him to repeat himself, "I don't understand my son he doesn't listen to me." As he repeated himself he heard what he was saying."

How often do we talk at people and believe we are communicating. I think it is particularly easy to fall into this trap with our children. When they are young it is easy to believe that we know best and we need to teach them how it is. What we now require is two way communication. Whenever we discuss something important with anyone, listening is generally the best way to start.

"Most people do not listen with the intent to understand; they listen with the intent to reply."
Stephen R. Covey, The 7 Habits of Highly Effective People: Powerful
  Lessons in Personal Change

When did you last really listen to your child? When you are planning your communication, it is necessary to plan in space to really listen without worrying what you are going to say in reply. Put down your thoughts for a moment and concentrate on their words. When you have listened to someone it can be helpful to repeat what you think you heard.

You might say something like, "what I heard is that you are really worried about….." Use their words as much as you can. Wait until your child feels heard before you go on to state what you have to say.

SAY WHAT YOU NEED TO SAY

Know what you want to say and explain why you are saying it. If it is about your child then make sure they are clear about your motivation. If you have listened respectfully to your child they may listen to you. If they interrupt, politely ask if you can finish, reassuring them that you will listen to them again in a moment.

LISTEN AGAIN

If your child has more to say then listen, really listen again. Allow this interchange to go on respectfully until you feel that both of you have said what needs to be said.

AGREE

Whatever you have both said, agree or (conclude) on an outcome. It may simply be to disagree at this moment in time and come back together again another time to see if anything has changed for either of you or see if you can explore a different solution. It may be a decision just to try something for a few days. I have added the conclude, because whilst your child is very ill there are times that you need to simply state what you are going to do, because you have their best interests at heart. As they begin to recover it is better wherever possible to find a way in which you can both agree.

AN EXAMPLE PLAN

Situation	Where and when would be a good time?	When we have time on our own tomorrow morning we can go for a short walk.
Outcome	Why do I want to have this conversation?	I want to explain that I feel a need to stop talking to the anorexia because I don't feel it has Katharine's best interests at heart. I do want to listen to Katharine though.
State	How are you feeling?	You need to be in the right emotional state, don't start a serious conversation when you are angry, hurt or frustrated.
Listen	Ask a question then be quiet and listen	You seem to be very frightened/angry at meal times can you tell me about that?
Say	Say what you wish to say and why you are saying it.	I believe that it is anorexia telling you those horrible things. I am very worried about you and want you to get better so that you can be happy again. I really want to talk to you, but I have decided I am not going to argue with anorexia anymore because I don't think it has your best interests at heart. I am prepared to talk to Katharine but not anorexia.
Listen	Really listen.	
Agree or (conclude)	If possible find a way that you can agree in someway.	I hear that you don't agree with what I am saying, but can we agree that I am going to try this even if the anorexia doesn't like it.

GLOBAL STATEMENTS

Whenever you are communicating avoid global statements such as never, always, everyone. They can rarely be justified when you think about it there are few things that NEVER or ALWAYS happen. Be specific; it is easier for you to be believable and trustworthy when you are.

REASSURANCE

The structure I have written here is designed to support you; don't let it scare you. If you have considered all the things I have mentioned and you are coming from the place of an open heart your conversation will be worth having. The more you work through this, the more you will learn to trust your instincts. Take note of all of the above and then allow the conversation to flow by really being there with your child. More than anything, over time, having your complete attention and presence will begin to help them.

> *"The most precious gift we can offer anyone is our attention. When mindfulness embraces those we love, they will bloom like flowers"*
> Thich Nhat Hanh

TRUST

If you are to help significantly in your child's recovery you need to create an environment in which they feel they can trust you. They may not always like what you do or suggest, but if you are considerate you will be able to give them glimpses that you have their best interests at heart. This will only come, however ,if you are prepared to listen to them. In order for you to be able to help your child it is actually more important for them to feel heard than for you tell them what you think. When you have agreed to do something then it is important that you stick to it. Don't say one thing and do another. You may not be able to trust the anorexia. The fact that Katharine often lied to us as a result of her anorexia caused her much distress, but that was not a reason for me to behave in an untrustworthy manner. Your child absolutely needs to see that you keep to your word. They are currently likely to trust the anorexia more than you, so don't give them grounds to doubt you. Don't promise things you can't do, but do keep any promises you make.

MANAGE YOUR EXPECTATIONS - THIS ISN'T GOING TO BE EASY

Talking to Katharine recently, she told me that when I first started refusing to talk to the anorexia, she said she hated it. It made her really frustrated. "It felt like you wouldn't talk to me, I couldn't separate myself, the anorexia was me, it was my voice, it sounded like me and your refusal to talk to it meant I couldn't say anything." She went on to say that, "now I can see it was important and it did help in the long run, but I hated it at the time."

This is why the things that we talked about in Chapter Six are so critical. You need to know how much you love your child and why you are doing this, you need to find the strength to fight for the future. If you are clear in your own mind, the tough love that you give will pay off. Work on your own thoughts and clarity. That is what is going to help your child the most.

It is not that likely that your child is going to like these changes. Trust that over time they will make a difference. You are working here with something that is very ingrained. It is going to take time and patience. Every time you try to talk, learn from it. Notice what worked, notice what seemed a disaster. Pat yourself on the back for trying. It is really important that through this struggle you acknowledge what you are doing. You are making a difference even if you can't see it now. Your relationship with your child will be so much better and so much stronger than it has ever been. They are unlikely to be able to see or acknowledge that now; in fact in the beginning they are likely to really hate this change. When you want to help them and start implementing strategies to do so, the anorexia is going to get threatened. This means that things could get worse before they get better, but trust the process.

Plan and practise. Be really kind to yourself. You are on a difficult journey, but you can do this and you can make a difference. Most people aren't prepared to take on the level of responsibility you are taking on here, but that is why your outcome is going to be good.

"At first I did fight my mum's "techniques," the idea that the

voice in my head controlling me was not actually part of me....because how could that possibly make sense? She challenged it, which made it stronger, I resented her for it, I fought her, but she didn't give up. I really, really hope you are able to try this. Don't stop because you don't want the fight, you're not really fighting with your child. You've got to be cruel to be kind I guess, and it's tough, it was so tough for all of us. As much as I hated my mum at the time, the bond we have now is so much stronger because of what we went through together. She showed me the potential of an easier way of life, that I didn't have to live like that and now I don't."

CHAPTER SUMMARY

In this chapter I have asked you to notice that you have a voice in your head that isn't you. I have explained that the anorexic voice in your child's head is constantly bullying them, at the moment it is this bully they listen to. I have asked you to start distinguishing between your child and the anorexia voice. Your child is not the anorexia. We have explored things that you might want to say and how to plan for effective conversations. I have outlined the importance of you being trustworthy and encouraged you not to get disheartened.

ACTION POINTS FOR YOU
- Be aware of your own brain chatter. Start noticing your own internal conversations.
- Look for distinctions between your child and anorexic conversations or behaviours. You may want to write down the characteristics of both, how do you see your child, how do you see the anorexia.
- Think and make notes on what you might want to say and the questions you might want to ask your child.
- Create a safe space to talk (physically and emotionally).
- Make some time to listen to your child.
- Start not listening to the anorexia and communicating with your

child differently.
- Make a note in your journal of how you are feeling and what is going on for you. This recognition will help as you go forward.
- Progress may seem so slow that day to day you may not see it, but over time this will help you.

ACTION POINTS FOR YOUR CHILD:
- How do you feel about your parents wanting to help you get better?
- How do you feel about the idea that you and anorexia are different?
- What are your feelings about getting better?

Ruth Steggles

Chapter 8

Looking to the Future

"Destiny is no matter of chance. It is a matter of choice. It is not a thing to be waited for, it is a thing to be achieved."

William Jennings Bryan

Ruth Steggles

TO RECOVER, YOUR CHILD NEEDS TO BELIEVE IN A FUTURE; YOUR JOB IS TO HELP THEM DO THAT.

WHAT THIS CHAPTER IS ALL ABOUT

In this chapter, I discuss ideas about how to help your child believe in their future. I have written them in the order that we used them and I explain how they helped us. I then go on to describe methods you can use to help change the mood and atmosphere for you and your family, creating a more positive environment for recovery.

HEALTH WARNING!

We are about to explore a number of ideas that can really help over time to make a difference to you, your child, their health and your relationship. They are presented in the order that we introduced them with Katharine. However, I would recommend that you choose the thing that speaks to you most and that you feel you could implement. Try one thing and then, when that feels like something you can keep up, gradually add in something else. There is no such thing as failure, only feedback; try something, find what works and what doesn't. Don't expect immediate results; keep going. Just by being here and giving things a go you are doing an amazing job. Professionals have the same approach, they have some tools that help some people, they try them with individuals and see if they work; if they don't they try something else. Not everything works for everyone but the underlying theme with all these tools is to get focused on a future and to find tools to create and sustain that belief whilst finding ways to cope emotionally with the experiences of life.

LOOKING TO THE FUTURE

When, as a family, we were first plunged into the depths and horror of anorexia, the future appeared very scary and was something I didn't really want to contemplate. There was so much fear and unknown about it for me that I didn't want to look at or think about it. The same is often true for the person suffering from anorexia. Anorexia is offering a useful, but short term solution for anyone suffering from it. Anorexia appears to offer a remedy for the sufferer for feelings and behaviours that are being experienced now. The internal rule book and ideas that have been constructed provide rules that, if applied now, will get them through the day. When we start to look to and believe in the future, we can start constructing ideas and pictures of how we would like it to be. When someone with anorexia starts to look to the future, over time they can begin to see that their visions and dreams would be far easier to achieve and better to experience without anorexia on their shoulder. So spending time creating future goals and pictures is a worthwhile investment.

One of the things that anorexia does for both someone suffering with it and the people that care about them is take away hope. One of the things we can do as a parent is help to build a vision of hope for the future.

You might currently be scared and not want to think about what the future might hold, but expecting good outcomes, and working on believing that they will happen, is essential to helping your child believe in a bright future. It may be really hard at this moment in time to believe that things will be alright, but practising the idea in your head or even getting to a stage where you are determined it will be that way are helpful. You having belief in the future will definitely help you to communicate this idea. I promise you that things can change and you can help your child find themselves once more if you are prepared to work with them.

I didn't really understand any of this at the time that I desperately needed to help Katharine, but I knew that I needed to do something and it was a massive relief for me when I came across the book Mom, please help – Karen Phillips. In which a mother with a daughter even sicker than Katharine found some strategies to help. For us, the "Who are you?" game was the first step on the road to recovery for the whole family.

THE "WHO ARE YOU?" GAME

I explained to Katharine that this exercise had been useful in helping another sufferer to get better. We found a quiet place where we could both sit and chat comfortably. Each time I had a note book to write in. We sometimes had a talk first, but often we would just play the game. I would ask her, "Who are you?" and write down the response. Thirty seconds later I would ask the same question, "Who are you?" and again write down Katharine's response. I repeated this a dozen or more times. The process was repeated by then asking, "Why are you here?" a dozen or so times and then finally, "What is your purpose?"

In the beginning, this seemed pointless and heart breaking. When I first asked Katharine who she was she had absolutely nothing to say. I just gave her space to reflect and think. Reassuring her occasionally that that was ok, just to think about it. After a number of sessions she came up with "me," then "I am a daughter," then another time "a sister" and eventually "a friend," "someone who cares." As time went on, she could boldly state who she was and I could see her regaining her identity.

I talked to Katharine about this recently, and what she now remembers as particularly useful was "what is your purpose?" By exploring that over time she found things she wanted to do and reasons she wanted to get better. We played this game for half an hour every day for months. All through the time in Spain and for several months afterwards. It became a bit of a ritual, just what we did. It built a safe place and even though at times Katharine didn't want to do it because it was boring, it did start to teach her subconscious that there was stuff she wanted to get better for and that there were things she wanted to do.

As you play the "Who are you?" game, you are helping your child to explore what the possibilities might be for them. You are discovering what is important to them. Helping build a future with the things they want, rather than the things you think they want, is powerful.

THE "WHO ARE YOU?" GAME

Who are you?	Repeat every 30 seconds about a dozen times.
Why are you here?	Repeat every 30 seconds about a dozen times.
What is your purpose?	Repeat every 30 seconds about a dozen times.

In general conversation, talking about your child's wishes for the future and their desires can be a pleasant distraction from the pressure of today and eating or not eating. If you hear anorexia coming into the conversation, "I want to be thin and beautiful……" just comment that that sounds like anorexia talking and you would rather not have the conversation with it. If it sounds like your child, but you hear they are scared or confused, reassurance might be what's needed. "I can't think about the future, there is no point……" You could empathise and also reassure. "I can see that it is really hard to believe that at the moment, but I know that with time you will be able to stop being bullied by the anorexia and there will be things that you want to achieve." Depending on their response you may want to remind them of things they talked about before they were ill.

VISION BOARDS

For Katharine's recovery one of the turning points was coming to believe that there was something worth living for. Life had become so miserable and frightening much of the time; there were many occasions when she didn't really see the point in going on or certainly in trying to get better. One of the exercises that I had done previously in a work context was to make a vision board. This can be a lovely exercise in looking to the future. We did it as a family and still have the results up around the house.

Vision boards can be great fun to create. Get a pile of magazines that you can cut up, some really big sheets of paper - we use big coloured poster size pieces - scissors and glue. Find a relaxing time and space. Maybe put on some music that you all enjoy. Flick through the magazines, tearing or cutting out anything that appeals to you, words or pictures. When you have a pile of torn out things, have a look at them and decide what you want to stick on the big sheet of paper to represent how you would like your future to look. Don't think too hard about it, just go with the flow. You will all be impressed by what you come up with. When you have finished your masterpiece you may wish to explain to the others what your images, words and pictures mean. It is up to you, but enjoy the process and then put it somewhere where you can look at it regularly. It can be a great way of goal setting.

I have used vision boards on a number of occasions in my life, and I am always amazed when I come back a few years later at how much of what is in my picture I have achieved. For the purpose of where you are at the moment, the important thing is the belief for you all that there are things for you to look forward to. That there will be a bright tomorrow. It will give your child an opportunity to explore what things they might like to do and achieve in their future. These strong images will give them something to focus on when they are battling with anorexia.

GOAL SETTING

As your child's ideas about the future grow and they begin to see there are actually things they want to do and achieve, encourage them to record or express these things. Having a goal book, or writing in a journal what they want to do and what it is going to be like. In the beginning it may be really hard for them to believe these things and it may frighten the anorexia. Just reassure them that with time and help they can be or do whatever they want. There is no right or wrong way to write or record goals, but recording them in some way, seeing them regularly and practise believing in them is incredibly helpful.

AFFIRMATIONS

In your child's recovery, you are supporting change. They have been behaving and believing certain patterns for some time. This means that effort is going to be needed for change. Affirmations can be very helpful in this process.

After we had played the "Who are you?" game for a little while, and Katharine began to have something to say (in the beginning she really had nothing to say), I encouraged her to spend a little time writing some affirmations. Affirmations are simply statements, written or spoken, of things that we would like to be. By regular repetition over a period of time we can train our brains to believe they are true. In the beginning we may not believe them but with persistence we can start to convince ourselves of their validity. In Mom Please Help, Karen suggested creating two columns on a page. In the column on the right hand side write a positive affirmation, and on the left hand side write the response that comes up for you from your brain.

Here is an example of what Katharine wrote:

I can happily eat as much as I want and still be the perfect weight – You'll put on weight
I can happily eat as much as I want and still be the perfect weight – What I want to eat is too much
I can happily eat as much as I want and still be the perfect weight – I need to burn off everything I eat

Katharine did these exercises repeatedly for a short while. The more she wrote them, the more she attached to the affirmation and let go of the counter argument.

"I am choosing to be healthy" is another one she wrote.

Katharine didn't much like doing this and it did take a bit of persuasion. I have used affirmations at various times in my life and found them helpful. Particularly in circumstances where I felt insecure or in need of courage. "I can do this and everything is happening perfectly" has stood me in good stead on a number of occasions. Whist writing can be more powerful, the habit of saying them is not without merit. It may be a helpful habit for you as well as to encourage your child to do. State things the way you want them to be, practise this statement, allow the doubting voice to speak its peace, but you don't have to listen. Start picturing, hearing, feeling your affirmations. Over time we can come to believe them and with that belief comes actions that lead to their fulfilment.

"I AM GREAT" GAME

Recently I was with a bunch of friends and we discovered how bad we were at stating what we are good at. We challenged one another to boldly state, "I am great at......." I have since played this with Katharine when we were out walking. It was a perfect way to explore the things we rarely acknowledge in ourselves, to make suggestions to the other person about what they are good at and to really step in to our gifts. Had I thought about it earlier I think it would have been perfect to introduce this during

Katharine's recovery. We are all good at some things and it benefits us all to know and accept that.

LAUGHTER

It can be hard to laugh when life is tough. It is hard sometimes to find things even to smile about when you feel you have the weight of the world on your shoulders but laughter has strong psychological and physiological effects. Watching a funny movie together regularly, reading funny stories, or finding good jokes will really help everyone. Find things that you have always enjoyed as a family, that have made you laugh, and make a positive effort to include these regularly in your schedule. We got into the habit of watching a funny movie together as a family every Friday night. Not only did it bring humour to our lives, it brought some consistency and a level of connection. Again this is really simple, but vitally important. It will put moments of normality into an otherwise fraught life. The more ways you can bring laughter into your lives the better. It will help the healing for all of you.

BOOKS, REALITY AND CONSISTENCY

I have always been solution orientated. If there was a problem I wanted to solve it, and here I was with a big problem, so I had already committed to the idea that I was going to do whatever I could to make a difference to Katharine. Whenever I came across an idea that I thought might be helpful or just something to have a go with, I would read it in a book, picture it in my mind, think about what I would say and how it would all go and how helpful it would be. I would get excited that this particular idea could really make a difference and with the little bit of preparation I would plough on in. Nine times out of ten, it would be a big belly flop, Katharine would be resentful, refuse to talk, get cross, slam doors or we would row. I would feel deflated, useless and frustrated. It had seemed so simple when I read it and yet when I put it into practice it was so hard. She didn't want to hear and I didn't feel good enough to make a difference. I am telling you this not to deflate you but to prepare you. The first time you try any of these things if you get as far as doing what you want it is unlikely that you will feel like you have had any success initially. If it doesn't end in some kind of altercation or resistance you are ahead of the curve, so please acknowledge your success. The key is to persevere.

You have some skills now; you need to believe in yourself and keep going. Everybody has the ability to think and behave differently, but in order to do so we have to overcome at the very least many months of habits and a particular way of being or thinking. The only way that we can make a real difference to automatic responses in the brain is to create new ones and that takes time, perseverance and consistency. Repetition, repetition, repetition.

CHAPTER SUMMARY
We have looked at ways to picture, imagine, and believe in the future. Having this focus will create hope for you all. We have looked at goal setting, affirmations and re-introducing laughter into your life. Finally I have encouraged you to keep going and trust that, if you do, the process it will work.

ACTION POINTS FOR YOU
- Start believing in the future.
- Plan some way of regularly thinking about the future (The "Who are you?" game worked for us!).
- Be persistent.
- Find ways of injecting humour into life for all of you – watch funny movies!
- Keep writing in your journal what you plan to do, noting what responses you get and anything you want to try differently.

ACTION POINTS FOR YOUR CHILD
- Whenever you can, start thinking about the future; what would you really like to do or achieve?
- Start collecting pictures of things that show what you want your life to be like.
- Talk to someone you trust about your dreams and maybe your fears.

Chapter 9

Self-Care, Maintenance and Support

"The perfect man of old looked after himself before looking to help others"

Chuang Tzu

Ruth Steggles

YOU NEED TO PUT YOUR OWN OXYGEN MASK ON FIRST SO THAT YOU ARE ABLE TO DO EVERYTHING THAT IS REQUIRED OF YOU NOW.

WHAT THIS CHAPTER IS ALL ABOUT

In this chapter I take you through ways of looking after yourself, so that you will be fit to help your child and the rest of the family. I encourage you to find the right people to support you, to take time for you, and for your other relationships. We look at helping you to connect to your natural environment and at some mindfulness techniques that will benefit you and your child.

LOOKING AFTER YOU

If you are anything like I was, your life has become so dominated by anorexia and a need to keep everything together for everyone else that your needs have come pretty far down the list. I am here to tell you that this is not sustainable long term. This is likely to be a long haul and you need to make sure that you are doing things to support you and that you create a support network for yourself. Much like when they tell you on an aeroplane in case of emergency, "put your own oxygen mask on first," you need to make sure you have the things you need to keep you breathing, in order that you can be of any help to the people around you. Not least your child.

WHAT DO YOU NEED?

Spend a bit of time thinking about something you have always loved to do. Draw, sing, dance, go out with friends. Whatever it is, find a way that you can fit some of that into your life. I am not suggesting running away and hiding, but I am talking about regularly just having an hour to do something you want to do for you. That time and space will fill you up and enable you to keep going. During Katharine's illness I went to a parents support group, and every woman in the room had given stuff up to cope with their child's illness, whether it was their work or their running or some other pastime. I completely understand how this happens, but don't lose yourself completely, enjoy reading a good book or having a dance. These things will elevate your mood and support everyone around you.

TEAM

What help, support and advice do you need around you? You can't shoulder this all on your own. I had a couple of great friends I could say anything to without any judgement, and whilst occasionally I would off load, mostly it was nice just to have somewhere to go and talk about normal things. I had the support of two nurses on our local CIT team and they were invaluable. One was a nurse assigned to Katharine whom I could talk to, but one nurse came to see me weekly and I know life would have been so much harder without him. To me it just felt like a safety net where I could voice all my concerns and worries. Whilst I was never really told what to do in these sessions, being able to talk through my thoughts, feelings and fears was massive for me.

It is really common for families where there is an eating disorder to isolate themselves. Prior to Katharine's illness we were fairly sociable, but most of our socialising involved food in some shape or form. As food became an issue and so stressful,l we found it easier just not to see our friends. The anorexia also seemed to take up so much of our time, with the anxiety from one meal stretching into the stress about the next. Whilst isolating yourself from the people you used to spend most time with is understandable, it is not the most helpful thing to do.

Other parts of your life might benefit from support. If you are devoting more time to your child, are there practical things that someone else can do for you. The truth is that people around you do know there is something wrong, even if you try and hide it, and mostly people want to help. If there are things that someone else could help with then ask. They will be glad you did, whether it is mowing your lawn, doing your ironing or taking your other children out to the park for an ice cream. All those things can make a difference. At times of stress we are designed to seek help; isolating yourself is the least useful thing you can do.

TIME AS A COUPLE AND AS A FAMILY

When anorexia invades your family it is hard to make time for anything. It is so easy to become completely absorbed in daily survival. Recognising the need for time together as a couple and for other family members is key. With the pressures around you it is easy for these things to become seemingly unimportant. I am always shocked at how much time slipped through our fingers whist Katharine was ill; if you don't make a conscious effort to put some time in with the important people in your life, you could wake up one day and find that you haven't spent any time with your husband or your other children in three years. Ask someone to come in and just be around while you and your partner go out together. Take it in turns to spend some time in the park with your other children one at a time; they are likely to appreciate having a bit of your undivided attention. You can use your new listening skills to really listen to anything they need to say. Sharing time with these other important people will make the journey easier for everyone.

Having time when your child with anorexia is not the centre of attention is good for everyone. The other people in your life will continue to feel valued and it will take the pressure off this child for a while.

WALKING

I have always been a walker to some extent, always enjoying being outside, and prior to Katharine's illness I did a bit of jogging. As a coach, I now do all my coaching while walking outside with clients. Whether it is something you have done in the past or something you have never thought of I recommend it as part of the recovery process for both you and your child.

We are designed to move and there is lots of research about the benefits of walking for both physical and mental wellbeing. Given that you are in a situation where there is potentially a lot of mental stress and your own welfare may be down the list of priorities, walking regularly will help you on many levels. It doesn't really matter where you walk, but if you can find any green space or water near to where you live, go there when you can and walk. Give yourself the time and the head space. I see - on an almost daily basis - my clients reaping the rewards of walking outside in a natural environment. Most of us have been suffering a massive disconnect from nature, travelling from brick boxes, in metal boxes to concrete boxes and back again in the same way. When I take people outside, a magic happens and they are supported in a way that I don't see people experiencing inside. I can understand that, sitting here with all the problems you are currently facing, this may seem trivial and way down the list of things you ought to be doing right now, but trust me and try it. You will find it provides support, connection and space if you let it. Outside is a great place to spend time with all the important people in your life as well as on your own. For me this is one of the fundamentals of the process.

SAFETY FIRST!

I want to stress here if your child is severely under-weight and bed rest has been prescribed, it is NOT appropriate to take her out walking. People with extreme weight loss may have put their heart under stress and a heart attack is possible in some cases. That said, if your child is under bed rest at home, and the temperature allows it, a little sitting in the garden or a park is likely to elevate their mood. Being in nature is very restorative for everyone.

EXERCISE AND WALKING

One of the precipitating factors in Katharine's illness was certainly over exercising, something she had become very dependent on in the development of her illness. In the early stages when we were trying to encourage her to eat, we did allow some exercise as a reward for her doing as we asked and consuming some food. I understand completely that this was contentious, but sport had become such an important part of what she did that it was hard to take it away from her completely. The medical professionals not directly involved in her care were very keen to remove all forms of exercise. I did however insist that she be allowed to keep walking as I could see the massive mental relief it gave her.

I understand that many people with anorexia are keen to walk long and fast and burn as many calories as possible. Katharine admits to me now that she would look forward to her walks because they were exercise, but that when she got out there it actually felt quite different. I could see and understand clearly that when Katharine was out walking she got some head space. Remember that with anorexia the sufferer has a voice talking and bullying them all the time, scaring them, nagging them. When Katharine went out walking she got a little bit of peace, a little bit of quiet in her head.

KEEP IT SLOW

We often walked together. This meant that I could keep it to a reasonable pace and limit the distance. Sometimes we would take the opportunity to chat and sometimes just be. Talking whilst walking is a very non-threatening non- aggressive way to converse. The fact that you are beside someone instead of facing them can often improve communication. It is a great opportunity for listening.

SOME WAYS IT WORKS

In my coaching work I have come across research showing that walking has similar attributes to EFT (Emotional Freedom Technique or Tapping) and hypnosis. Because of the bilateral movement (using both sides of one's body) it engages both sides of the brain. This has been found to have a beneficial effect on stress and trauma. What I saw in Katharine, and now see in my coaching clients, is that walking outside helps to clear the brain, helps people become more present and creative. All these things are good for someone whose brain is working overtime telling unhelpful stories.

So whilst most of the time I tried to accompany Katharine, on occasion I just let her go knowing that the few hundred calories that she might burn whilst out could be worth the sacrifice for the relaxation and brain space she would get as a result.

CLEAR YOUR HEAD

I would encourage you to use walking for both you and your child. Ideally in a green space, as I personally believe that connection with our natural environment helps to support and restore us. Gentle walking together, sharing some pleasant time, will serve you both. When you are looking for some space for yourself, 20 minutes' brisk walking will really help you clear your brain. Sometimes walk alone and sometimes share it with someone you can talk to honestly. These practices will help you not just now but for the rest of your life. For more information on the benefits of walking see "Walking your Blues Away" Tom Hartlan.

"Because I rebelled so strongly against any form of medical help, with its association of illness, my mum was the one

person who helped me through. If it wasn't for my mum, I don't like to think where I would be today. She gave me the strength to change my thought processes and actually start living again. The bond we share now is so special, I believe we both learned and gained in a certain way from what we went through; my hope for you is that you are able to do the same. Walking for me was a major help, at first the idea of going for walks appealed to the ill part in my brain, "Walking equals calories burned," which is ridiculous as even when I was trying to gain weight, this was a bonus. However, as soon as we actually got outside, so much weight was lifted from my mind, I became logical, my thoughts unclouded. Walking outside enabled me to put things into perspective, to access the stupidity of the whole situation. In moments of clarity like these, I realised that I couldn't, wouldn't, live my life like this. As a result of the techniques and time me and my mum spent together discussing and challenging this stubborn part of my brain, the more and more moments of clarity I would get. She helped me fight it into submission so I was me more of the time and in a better position to recover physically as well as mentally. I can now see that being outside is being away from the external noise and stimuli of society, it's a place where you can just be, where inner thoughts can be voiced rather than supressed."

TRUST AND SPACE

If you are have started attempting some of the things in the last few chapters you are starting on the road to recovery. With your support, belief, help and communication your child is going to get better. In Chapter 11, I shall talk about some of the practicalities of dealing with anorexia, but as long as your child is in no immediate danger it is ok to give them a bit of space. They need to learn over time to deal with their own space and you need some too. So, two things: trust the process, and allow some space for you and your child. If they are old enough and they haven't ever threatened to hurt themselves, it is ok to leave them alone occasionally.

MINDFULNESS AND MEDITATION
There is a lot written these days about mindfulness and meditation, but it wasn't something I had really paid much attention to before Katharine's illness. I came across it whilst looking for ways to help Katharine. She used some meditation tapes a little when she was ill and at the time I remember her commenting that they were useful. She no longer uses either, but I believe them to be an invaluable tool for both you and your child. Once again I think that if you want to suggest they do something, I think it is worth you giving it a try. If you visit my website: www.thefreshaircoach.co.uk on the page about Parenting and Anorexia there are a couple of meditations you can download for you and your child.

PEACE IS FOUND IN THE PRESENT MOMENT
Much of the pain we experience is based either on things that have happened in the past or things that may or may not happen in the future. In the brain of someone suffering with anorexia much of the stress and anxiety is about fear about the future, "if I eat that this will happen," or, "if I don't do that then such and such will happen." Mostly about unknown stuff in the future. I suspect a lot of the stress in your own mind is about things that may or may not happen at some time beyond this very moment. It is important, in the healing process, to be forward focused in a positive manner, but allowing some time to be completely present in this exact moment allows us to find a pause in the whirl of emotions we are experiencing. When we spend time in this exact moment, just being and witnessing what is, we can find some peace. For someone with an anorexic voice in their head, finding peace even for a moment is huge.

THE DIFFERENCE BETWEEN MINDFULNESS AND MEDITATION
Mindfulness and meditation are often used interchangeably, for me the distinction is that mindfulness is a kind of informal practice that one can carry out as part of daily life, and meditation is a more formal practice

that we need to put a side a small amount of time be it three minutes, 10 minutes, half an hour or an hour.

I am going to give you a brief description of a couple of techniques you could try. If this is something that appeals to you I recommend that you go to your library or Amazon and explore what is available. A great starting point is Mindfulness – Mark Williams and Danny Penman.

A SIMPLE MINDFULNESS EXERCISE
I like to do this walking, but you can do it whilst carrying out any activity like washing up. Engage each of your senses in turn, observing but with no judgement. So as you walk what do you see? Looking all around, what is in front of you, what is above you, what is below you, what is to your right, to your left and what is behind you? Just walk and notice. Then bring in your hearing what can you hear. Make no judgement; if, say, there are birds singing and traffic noise, just notice everything, don't have a commentary that the birds are beautiful and the traffic horrible, just be aware and notice. Now what can you taste and smell, then what are you feeling, first externally; what is the surface like under your feet, the feel of the fabric of your clothes on your skin, the breeze or sun on your face? Now go internally and starting at your feet work up your body, just noticing any sensations you are experiencing as you walk.

WASHING UP
You may choose to do it whilst washing up. Watch the water flowing into the sink, look at the colour and texture of how it hits the sink. What noise does it make? What are the bubbles of the washing up liquid like? What does the soap and water feel like on your skin?

It is possible that quite quickly your mind will disappear off somewhere else. When you notice that, just bring yourself back to the water or the dishes, noticing what it feels like, looks like, sounds like. Just try it, no judgement, and do it for a few minutes. The more you practise, the longer you will be able to sustain concentration.

These kinds of practices bring you completely into the present moment. They give you respite from the stuff of life and over time you learn to be in the present more and more. Eventually you will find that you are in a happier place. As a result of your learning to do this, your child has an opportunity to do the same and it will help you both.

A NOTE ON MEDITATION

Lots of people say to me that they can't meditate, their mind is too full, that it is difficult and they can't do it. Well I can't do 30 press ups straight at the moment, I can maybe do one or two. However I know that if I practised daily over time I would be able to do five and then 10 and I suspect work up to 30. Meditation is the same; not many people could sit for an hour with a calm mind without practice. It is also important to stress that there is no wrong practice; don't judge yourself in any of this. This book is not the time or place to discuss meditation in any depth. There are many books written on the subject; suffice to say the physical and mental benefits of meditation are more numerous than you can imagine, and only a few minutes a day will start to make a big difference. Given that you are in a very stressful situation, just taking five to ten minutes twice a day for the following exercise will really benefit you. Our children respond far more to what we do than what we tell them to do. I felt very much that I could serve Katharine by leading by example. This isn't something that she does regularly, but she did dip into it during her illness and now she does occasionally use guided meditations to give her a bit of head space and peace.

PREPARING TO MEDITATE.

I recommend just finding somewhere quiet where you know you won't be disturbed (I get that this is a challenge). It doesn't matter whether you sit or lie, the only important thing is that your spine is straight, by which I mean it is in line and allowed to have its natural gentle curve whilst you sit upright or lie (no slouching or twisting). I recommend that you do it in the same time slot every day as this helps to make it a habit. I meditate in my bedroom for 10 minutes every morning and in bed at night. Create your space and your time and then close your eyes, allow yourself a few moments to settle down.

A SIMPLE BREATHING MEDITATION

One of the simplest ways to meditate is to breath count. Find somewhere to focus on your breath. Classically it is to focus on the exact point that breath comes in and out of your nostrils. Breathe in through your nostrils and on the out breath count one. Breathe in again and on the out breath count two. If you find your mind wonders off to think about something, just notice it and bring your attention back to your breath and start again. Do a few cycles trying to count up to four, seven or 10. Before you try you may think that keeping your attention counting to four sounds very simple. Try it. In the whole process do not judge or criticise yourself, don't give yourself a commentary on how good or bad you are, just follow your breath and count. If your attention drifts just notice, bring your attention back to the tip of your nostrils watching your breath and start again.

If you have been practising affirmations as we discussed in Chapter Eight, you may like to repeat your own affirmation three times at the beginning and end of your session.

I would encourage you to explore over time other resources, such as other books, groups or courses, to fully appreciate the amazing benefits of meditation. Maybe it is an exciting adventure you will be able to explore with your child at some point. For the moment though, this simple practice will really support you to create the space and mental resources you need to serve yourself to be able to help your child. I know it may feel as if you don't have the time or energy to do this for yourself, but doing it will help you make time for the rest of life. I love this quote

"I have so much to accomplish today that I must meditate for two hours instead of one."
Gandhi

CHAPTER SUMMARY
In this chapter I have addressed the need for you to find ways in which to nurture yourself and find support. I have explained how important I believe it is to get out into nature, and how you might introduce some mindfulness and meditation into your routines.

ACTION POINTS FOR YOU

- Start being aware of yourself and looking after your own needs.
- Make sure you allow other people to help; who do you need on your team? Is there anyone missing?
- Spend time with other people in your immediate family.
- Get outside and walk.
- Try some mindfulness or meditation practice.

ACTION POINTS FOR YOUR CHILD

- See if you can find something that helps you relax.
- Try some of the meditation techniques that I have suggested

Ruth Steggles

Chapter 10

Thoughts, Language, Feelings and Communication

"Love is the absence of judgement."

Dali Lama

Ruth Steggles

IN ORDER TO CHANGE OUR REALITY WE NEED TO CHANGE OUR THOUGHTS, LANGUAGE AND FEELINGS.

WHAT THIS CHAPTER IS ALL ABOUT

In this chapter we explore ways in which we can change our thinking patterns by looking at our language and our feelings. We will look at how the simple practice of gratitude can change how we think and feel. We will look at ways to change our language, and ways in which acknowledging our feelings allows us to experience things differently. We all speak and think in ways that are largely a matter of habit. Your child has slipped into patterns of thinking that will certainly have served a purpose for them in the beginning. By looking at how we have been communicating and perhaps changing some of the ways we think and the things we say, we can help our child to create more useful patterns.

GRATITUDE

When people are struggling with life, let alone anxiety, depression or an eating disorder (which may already be a combination of these things), gratitude is an immensely helpful tool, and something I believe everyone should practise. When it has become something you do, then you can encourage your child to do the same. What I mean by gratitude is finding and recognising things that you have got to be grateful for. It is possible that, where you are right now, it feels really difficult to find things you are grateful for. You might be able to appreciate something as simple as the fact that you actually had three hours' good sleep last night; a delicious cup of tea; or that you are learning ideas to help your child. It doesn't matter how small the thing or experience is, find three things to say thank you for.

MAKE IT A HABIT

I would encourage you to make this a formal practice, so that either first thing in the morning or last thing at night you write down three things you are grateful for. As you start to do this, you may find that during the day you find more things to appreciate. The more you do this, the more your brain starts to change and the more you find to say thank you for. This starts to give you a more positive disposition. You are training your brain to find good things; don't try hard, don't manipulate things, just notice that beautiful flower or a friend giving you a call. By doing this yourself you can actively encourage your child to do so as well. Don't expect them to take on things you are not prepared to do: Start yourself and they are more likely to follow.

This is so simple you may think it is not worth bothering with. Please trust me that this is a life changing habit. Simple to do but simple not to do, so commit to it!

PERFECTION

Before we talk about language I want to consider the word perfection. Wikipedia defines it as:, broadly, a state of completeness and flawlessness. In Part One I referred to the "perfect" daughter, because I heard other people using it to describe their child before anorexia. It can be used as a very demanding word and places an unrealistic expectation whenever it is used. There is nothing that is flawless. The use of the word "perfect" in association with anyone suffering from anorexia is very dangerous. It is not un-common for personalities that strive to be the best to suffer from eating disorders. A desire to be better, thinner, or more, can precipitate this condition. We are all perfect in that we are complete, but I think it is a very dangerous word to use in relation to anything and certainly in this particular situation.

POSITIVE LANGUAGE

You have got to believe in the future, you have got to believe or act as if you believe everything is going to be alright. One of the ways of doing this is to change your language. Stop using negative words, talk about the things that can happen, not the things that can't.

When you talk about anything what sort of words do you use? Do you tend to comment on things you see going well or are you noticing what is going wrong and what isn't working? Do you compliment people or do you tend to notice what they haven't done? Do you talk about what you wish had happened or do you acknowledge and appreciate the tiny things that have gone well? Do you use powerful words or nondescript words? The language we use in our daily life affects the way we feel, our body language, the things we do and how we show up. The language in our head is often of a similar tone to the language we speak. When we talk more kindly and more positively externally it also improves our internal conversations. When we surround our families with positive words externally there is more chance they will be able to have more positive internal conversations. Here are some examples of negative conversations and positive comments:

Negative comments	Positive comments
I prefer the other one.	That is a good choice.
That was a bit quick should you have taken longer.	Well done you have achieved that faster than I expected.
I wish you hadn't done that.	Thank you I appreciate that.
I suppose I could if I really must.	That would be great – my pleasure.
I guess that is as good as it gets.	That's great.
Raining again!	I love the rain.
What do you expect, miracles?!	I am so pleased you are expecting great things.
It would have been good if…..	I am glad that.
Of course I haven't, what do you expect?!	I chose not to.
I don't much like that one.	I prefer this, thanks.
She isn't very clever.	Isn't she a really kind person?
Shame she can't sing though.	I love _____ about her.
Do you remember how awful……	What I really like was…

LETTING GO

Some of our negative language revolves about a need to control how things happen. Sometimes a feeling that our way is the best way or the only way. When we start examining what we are saying we may find a need to let go and trust that other people can do things as well. When we let go it can be scary but over time it can be very rewarding. When we cease to practise the illusion of control we find that the people around us become far more capable and supportive.

POWERFUL WORDS AND PHRASES

"I can do anything," "I believe it," "I feel great," "I am grateful," "I'm excited," "It's amazing," It's wonderful".......
Love, joy, happiness, peace, freedom, belief, trust, wisdom, energy, abundance, honesty, kindness....

This may all seem really false to you and a waste of time. But start noticing what you say and how you say it. I'm not asking you to lie in any way, but I am asking you to look to notice if there is another way of viewing something, a more empowering way to say something. It is possible that you don't know many people who speak in this way. Seek them out if you can, but if not have the courage to start making changes. Practise and learn. Make a list of words that really feel powerful and positive to you. Start using them in your daily conversations. Say things that empower you and the people around you.

FEELINGS

You may have noticed that we haven't talked about food at all yet and given that anorexia is an eating disorder that might surprise you. What we have been talking about is how you think and how you feel. I don't believe that sufferers find themselves with an eating disorder intentionally; somewhere along the line their feelings and emotions have become unbalanced or obsessive. This may be because inherently they have never been good at dealing with their feelings, through genetics or learnt behaviour, but whatever the background, anorexia has made feelings and emotions difficult to deal with. An inability to express or deal with feelings can be one of the underlying factors in the precipitation or continuation of eating disorders. Finding ways to acknowledge and express feelings is helpful. I have already talked about acknowledging your own feelings; becoming more aware of what goes on for you will help in your communication with your child.

In our case, Katharine and I got to a place where we talked a lot and this was the main way in which she was able to express and experience her emotions. However, not everyone feels able to talk and below are some ideas as to how emotions can be explored.

ACKNOWLEDGING FEELINGS

If your child is not ready to look to the future beyond playing the "Who are you?" game, exploring where they are now can be helpful. Using the same idea as I suggested with vision boards is one way to allow her to express her feelings. Cutting out images, words or colour to show how things feel at the moment and then sticking them on a bit of paper to make a collage is useful way of exploring emotions. Acknowledging feelings in an atmosphere of acceptance and non- judgement is really helpful, and one of the reasons I have asked you to explore your own feelings on this journey.

In my own journey and as a coach I have seen that acknowledging feelings and allowing them is far healthier than supressing them. Finding ways to let them out safely is really helpful. If you or your child find this hard, there are a number of things you can encourage. Drawing, painting, playing an instrument (by which I don't mean mastering a skill, but banging a drum or shaking a tambourine in different ways to show different feelings), singing, shouting, journaling, are all ways of expressing emotion. Experiment and find what works for them. Simply beginning to accept that feelings are ok to experience and it really is a case of "better out than in." Giving yourself a means to express emotion is far less risky than supressing.

Our feelings are there to give us a bit of feedback. Expressing or acknowledging a feeling is simply a recognition, it doesn't mean it is permanent or going to stay that way for any length of time. In fact, often once a feeling has been acknowledged we are more able to let it go. Encouraging expression of feelings in a non-judgemental way is a good way to build trust. People need to be heard, and if you create space and ways in which your child feels heard they are more likely to trust you and learn to express themselves more. For a person who has been striving for "perfection," acknowledging feelings that may be labelled "bad" can be quite challenging.

EMOTIONAL FREEDOM TECHNIQUE (EFT) OR TAPPING

When Katharine was ill I read a little about EFT, but I didn't really understand enough about it to use it with her. Since that time I have used it a lot with clients and see it having an amazing positive effect. It is a really useful method of exploring and dealing with emotions. I am a huge fan. I am aware that I am throwing loads of ideas at you, but this is something you may wish to explore. There are practitioners including myself who can do this work with you or your child, but Nick Ortner has a website, www.thetappingsolution.com, that provides great video and resources if it is something that is safe to explore yourself.

BRING IT ON

My work as a coach means that I often examine things that frustrate me in order to re-frame them or think of them differently so as not to cause me distress. There are, however, still things that really do irritate me; I now practise what I call "bring it on." So if something has really upset me or is challenging me, rather than trying to stop it, I create some space to really feel whatever it is. I find somewhere I can just "be" for a few minutes and allow myself to feel whatever it is. I really open up to the experience and allow the emotions to flow, no judgement, just let them come and do whatever they want to do. It rarely lasts long and I always feel better afterwards. I sit and say to myself "bring it on" and let the emotions flow. What we resist persists and what we allow can flow away. Try these things yourself, because you will find that over time, as you get better at dealing with your own stuff, you will have more to offer your child. We lead our children more by what we do than by what we say. Start treating yourself well and over time they can learn to do the same for themselves.

WORD OF WARNING

I have mentioned journaling throughout this second part and I believe it can be very helpful for both you and your child; keeping a private diary of some sort or recording feelings is a useful thing to do. There are these days lots of online sites where people can blog or write public diaries (for my teenagers Tumblr was one of them). I would discourage this type of public activity. Whilst someone suffering from anorexia needs support, they need the right support, and they don't need commentary from an online public community where they may actually find support for their anorexic behaviour. If your child feels heard and supported at home, they may find less need for this broader public support.

Dealing with feelings is part of an on- going process. Whilst on this journey you need to be aware of and express feelings, but don't just stay where you are, talking about how you feel over and over again. Make sure you acknowledge what is going on, but practise letting go, using powerful language and gratitude to make sure that you are creating a positive state for you and your child.

CHAPTER SUMMARY
In this chapter I have talked about practising gratitude, noticing good things daily. I have explored ways in which you may choose to change your language to make it more supportive for you and the people around you. Finally I have suggested some ways in which you and your child might express some of the things you are feeling.

ACTION POINTS FOR YOU
- Practise gratitude daily.
- Spend some time looking at the language you use. Find more useful things you can say.
- Suggest ways your child might like to express how they are feeling.
- Do this for yourself.

ACTION POINTS FOR YOUR CHILD
- Practise finding things you are grateful for.
- Find a way to express your feelings; possibly keep a diary or a journal; make sounds/music; paint or draw or talk to someone you can trust.

Ruth Steggles

Chapter 11

Practicalities

"Don't try to solve serious matters in the middle of the night."

Philip K. Dick

Ruth Steggles

ASK QUESTIONS, BE PRACTICAL AND BE PREPARED.

WHAT THIS CHAPTER IS ALL ABOUT

This is the chapter I least wanted to write. The rest of the book is about healing and where you are going; it contains positive ideas of growth expansion and learning, that are going to take you to great places. I am now grateful for all the learning we had through the process of Katharine's recovery and we both have a sense that we have gained in ways that we couldn't have imagined. In this chapter I am going to explore ways to manage some of the daily challenges you have to face in order to achieve all the other things I have talked about. We are going to look at how to manage eating, food preparation and meal times. I encourage you to think about other critical areas such as the use of anti-depressants and whether or not weighing should be part of your child's treatment.

EATING

You may have noticed that we haven't talked about food yet, which may surprise you given that your child has an eating disorder. Their relationship with food is a symptom rather than a cause and the stuff we have covered so far will, over time, help to address the underlying cause. However, today it is important that your child receives enough nutrition in order to survive.

We have always had meal times together and I am aware that these days that is not necessarily the norm. It may be hard at the moment to start this if it would be a significant change for your family. If having joint meals is something you have never done then at the very least you may want to start planning to have meals yourself with your child. I believe that eating together is helpful. Don't get me wrong; I do understand that eating with anorexia at the table is not the most enjoyable of experiences, but your presence and support is helpful. Over time and as your child recovers, introducing family meal times can become a great opportunity to converse and share as a family.

PLANNING

Do not make the dinner table a battle field. In the early stages when your child is still likely to be very fearful of food, plan in advance what will be in a meal and what you expect they will eat. All planning, negotiation and discussion should be made well in advance and not near the table. Stay in charge, have the courage and conviction that you know what is best. Be firm but not cross and angry. If you are working with professionals on a diet plan you may want to bring their evidence into the discussion. Be clear, you can acknowledge your child's feelings, you can observe what they are feeling and try and articulate it to help them feel understood. "I can see that having to have a yoghurt as well today feels quite scary for you, but we have planned this to help you to get better. I am not going to allow you to get fat but I am helping you to get healthy. You will be able to do this today and I will be there for you." If you want to put in some room for negotiation then plan that in advance – "Would you like carrots or broccoli?" "Chicken or ham?" Choices should be equivalents, not entirely different: allowing a swap from cheese to cabbage is not helpful. Choice may make things too challenging, and it might actually be easier for your child in the early stages to have no choice at all. Over time as they begin to recover, allowing them some choice and gradually giving them more responsibility is part of the recovery, but too much too soon is likely to be counter-productive.

REWARDS

You may want to put in some kind of reward system. If you manage to eat what we have planned today, tomorrow we could arrange for you to go and….. Be realistic, if you do offer any sort of reward system then make sure it is sensible and achievable. Goals that feel too large or unachievable are more de-motivating than motivating.

Plan	Know in advance what you intend to prepare for a meal. Seek out dietary advice from professionals so you can be really confident about what she needs to eat.
State	Ideally you wouldn't have to tell them what is for tea, but if they ask just state it clearly.
Limit choice	Your child may try to negotiate; don't enter into arguments. In order that they feel they have some control you may want some choice over equivalents eg. broccoli or carrots?

Acknowledge emotions	Be supportive, acknowledge any emotions they seem to be feeling, but reassure them.
Stay firm	Don't negotiate with the anorexia; if you hear it arguing then stop and state that it sounds like that is anorexia talking and you only want to talk to your child.

"I think I will always have a tendency to be overly controlling around food; it's my way of coping in stressful situations and an underlying habit I guess. But now I can recognise it, I can see when I have an illogical thought, and I can question it, it doesn't control me. Again, I compare it to cancerous cells because I find that's an easier way to think of it. There is always the possibility that it could come back, I just know the early symptoms and how to deal with it before it gets out of hand and spreads."

PREPARATION

If possible, keep your child away from the preparation of food. This isn't so that you can hide a dollop of cream for extra calories; it is so that it is less stressful for both of you. Having them breathing over your shoulder won't help you, and contemplating the food won't help them. If you do manage to cook on your own I don't recommend that you do try and put a dollop of extra calories in without them seeing. Cook as you would normally; if you have always put butter in something then carry on doing so, but don't do it now because you think you could get away with it. In order to be able to work with your child, you need them to trust you. If they distrust you then it will be harder for you to help them make progress. Make your plans openly in advance and stick to them. If they really need to be in the kitchen and you feel that is an argument too far, then let them sit or stand away from you. Put on some good music and just try to chat about things completely unrelated to food.

THE DINNER TABLE

This may be really hard for your child. It is helpful to understand that. Thinking they are just being awkward is likely to make you less supportive. Create a pleasant environment. It can be helpful to have some relaxing music on in the background. Choose carefully though, because loud and energetic music could make the situation more stressful. Try and create surroundings that are as calm as possible. Be supportive, but expect that your child can eat what is planned. Try not to focus on the food or eating, you may want to chat about other things. Don't, however, allow your child to use this as a cue to not eat anything. Encourage them occasionally if that seems helpful. Trying to distract them from the internal dialogue about what they can and can't do may be helpful. If they articulate that they can't eat something then point out that that sounds like anorexia talking. Remind them that you had already planned together that eating what is in front of them is part of helping them be healthy. Everything on their plate is there to help them get better and you know they can do this. You understand this feels very hard, but you know they can do it.

Be prepared to let it take a while, but if they are not attempting to eat at all they may need encouragement and to be reminded of your previous agreements. When they have finished, stay at the table, or go and sit somewhere quietly together for a bit. This was often the time we chose to play the "Who are you?" game. In the time after a meal, your child is potentially vulnerable to negative internal conversation. Recognising this and spending some time with them at this point may be helpful. For those sufferers who are tempted to make themselves vomit, the first half an hour after a meal is the optimum time for them to get rid of food. Finding a way to distract your child or support them through this critical time is helpful.

Be strong and firm in your resolve. Remain calm and reiterate that everything you are doing is to help them become healthy so that they can do everything they want with their life. Tap into that feeling for yourself when it gets hard.

| Manage Your State | Remember everything we have talked about to stop you feeling stressed. Expect a positive outcome; anything else won't help. |
| Environment | Make wherever you eat pleasant. Sit at a table if possible; play relaxing music. |

Conversation	If possible chat about things unrelated to food. Do not negotiate with anorexia. Stick to the plan.
Afterwards	Recognise they may feel vulnerable. Spend some time, chat or maybe reassure them if they need it.

NUTRITION

I explained in Part One that on a couple of occasions Katharine was prescribed Ensure, a supplement drink which provides calories and nutrition. She found it helpful as it was a controlled number of calories and it helped her feel in control of what was going on. In the long term there is a need to move away from that need to control, but it certainly served a purpose at critical moments when she was very underweight.

Throughout the time that Katharine was ill, she took a supplement called Juice Plus that she had taken for a few years prior to her illness. She took these capsules of dehydrated fruit and vegetables daily. I have no idea whether they were of any major benefit to her, but I was surprised that, given how underweight she was for two years, she didn't suffer any other kind of illness. I mention it here as a point of information rather than a recommendation.

USE ALL THE HELP YOU CAN GET – BUT KNOW YOUR OUTCOMES

In the previous chapter I talked about team and I would actively encourage you to seek out all the professional help you can get. However, do not then hand over complete control assuming that you are going to get your child back well and recovered. To really make the most of whatever support is available, know what you want your outcomes to be. Ask questions, ask for ideas. I was constantly writing questions that I wanted to know the answer to. I discussed with Katharine what she wanted to know. Whenever we went to an appointment I went with a list of things I wanted to discuss. I know that if I hadn't written it down I would not have remembered or got answers to everything I wanted. Even though I am relatively confident, meetings in hospitals with doctors and other professionals often felt intimidating. I was good at telling myself they were judging me or had opinions of me (none of which I had any evidence for, but we are very good at doing this to ourselves when we feel vulnerable). Be prepared to be part of the team, listen and ask questions but also don't be afraid to make suggestions.

Value your own voice and opinions in these interactions. The professionals may have a lot more experience with anorexia in lots of people, but you are the expert on your child. It is helpful for everyone if you play your part, but most important for your child.

ANTI-DEPRESSANTS
It is not uncommon for anti-depressants to be prescribed to treat the inevitable negative emotions that come with anorexia. For many people this appears to be a good solution. My advice would be to think about it and ask questions. What are the benefits, and how will coming off them be managed? Are there other things that could be done instead? They were offered to Katharine on a couple of occasions, but for me they always needed to be an absolute last resort. Whilst I do understand that they have a physical effect on body chemistry, I personally believe there are often other ways in which these same affects can be achieved. The things that have been discussed in Chapters Eight, Nine and 10 may be worth trying for a while before the use of antidepressants. You need to explore what is right for you and your child. Learning tools and techniques that a person can have to hand for their whole life makes the most sense to me, but I do know of many people who have found anti-depressants helpful to them.

TO WEIGH OR NOT TO WEIGH?
I don't believe there is a right or wrong answer here and I raise the subject in order that you think about what your desired outcomes are. When someone is very ill with anorexia, it is often not possible to trust them as they are being so controlled by the anorexic voice. It may not be possible to tell what they are eating, and weighing someone is one way of observing what is happening. Be awareweighing can be distorted by hidden objects or water loading.

Katharine was weighed weekly. One of the nurses from our CIT team called in on their way to work. It was very stressful for Katharine on the lead up and in the aftermath. Whatever the outcome, there was always something to discuss about it. We used weighing to mark progress for myself and her team. We used it to set targets for her to aim for so that she could get back to the sport she loved. We could have monitored her health in other ways by measuring pulse and blood pressure. I absolutely accept it is extremely important to have some measure of a person's health in order to protect them, and if you have no guarantee of what is being consumed and whether it is staying down then measuring weight gain or loss is a good indicator of that, but be aware why you are doing it and don't necessarily do it for the sake of it.

In some ways Katharine's stress over pending weighing, weight gain or loss gave us a good opportunity to discuss how she was feeling and what that meant. So with appropriate awareness you can benefit from the situation. If, however, someone is too distressed by the weighing process, explore the possibility of weighing them without them seeing what the result is. It is far better to be weighed in a situation supported by someone else (either at a surgery, with a health professional or in a chemist) than having scales lying around at home where weighing could become an obsessive pastime for you or your child. As Katharine regained her health, the frequency of weighing was decreased.

"I dreaded those morning, "weighings." It was literally like the whole week built up to those moments. If I'd put on enough weight then I could potentially introduce one more activity, if I put on too much weight…well the possibility was too horrible to consider, even though I knew the quicker the better; there was nothing logical about it but the thought absolutely terrified me. The outcome of those sessions would then determine whether the week would be a positive or negative one. A weight loss was awful, every kg meant so much at this point, dragging on the painful process. I really don't think these aided my mental recovering at all; everything was so focused on the weight, which surely is not the important thing, if anything it fuelled the anorexia. It was another thing to be controlled; if I'd put on too much

weight I would need to lose weight again. It was just another battle that raged on in my head, completely exhausting. I absolutely despised those scales, and unfairly the doctor who brought them to me."

CHAPTER SUMMARY

In this chapter I have encouraged you to plan in advance the atmosphere and expectation around meal times. To take responsibility for your state and the atmosphere whilst eating. To be part of the team responsible for your child's recovery to explore and ask questions. To explore what you think is best for them and influence their journey back to wellness.

ACTION POINTS FOR YOU
- Plan meal times, their content and atmosphere.
- Plan and ask questions about your child's treatment plan (be part of it).
- Don't simply accept anti-depressants because they are suggested, without considering the implications.
- Consider what part weighing plays in recovery and how it can best be managed for your child's benefit.

ACTION POINTS (AND A NOTE) FOR YOUR CHILD
- Keep writing about your feelings.
- Express your opinions about your recovery.

If someone close to you has taken the trouble to read this book and is trying to put some of the things here into action, they do really care about you, even if it doesn't always feel like it. If they have got this far they do really want what is best for you. They want you to recover and they are doing their very best to help you. If you can try sometimes to trust them, and keep expressing how you feel, I honestly believe that over time you will fully recover and be able to create whatever life you want for yourself.

AND FINALLY

As a parent the fact that you have come this far shows a desire to help. You have more resources than you believe and you are enough. This is not your fault and you honestly have the power to make a difference. In this book I have shared lots of ideas with you and I really encourage you to explore them and work through them without judgement. Keep persevering. I most want to give you courage to really be part of your child's recovery and for you all to grow through the experience. I honour you for your commitment

AND FINALLY IN KATHARINE'S WORDS:

"I hope reading this book has given you a sense of hope, because there is most definitely hope. Don't give up on your child or that hope."

I wish you all the very best on your journey; my thoughts, love and support are with you all!

I learned that courage was not the absence of fear, but the triumph over it. The brave man is not he who does not feel afraid, but he who conquers that fear.
Nelson Mandela

Ruth Steggles

Further Help and Feedback

GETTING IN TOUCH

Ruth has coached in her direct selling business for fifteen years, supporting people to build a business that fitted in with their family life and other commitments. The self–development she explored through that gave her a grounding to help Katharine when she first became ill. The experience they shared led Ruth to take a coaching qualification and she has been working with individuals and groups ever since. If you would like to explore working with Ruth to support you, your family or someone else you know then please get in touch.

We also really appreciate your feedback as this helps improve the process for others. Please ask questions and give us your comments.

You can visit Ruth's website:
www.thefreshaircoach.co.uk

or e-mail Ruth:
ruth@thefreshaircoach.co.uk

Ruth Steggles

Epilogue

SOME OF KATHARINE'S THOUGHTS NOW

"In the midst of my illness, when my mind wasn't occupied with thoughts of food and exercise, I would often focus on the unfairness of my situation. However, recovering from anorexia has been an undeniable learning curve; my experiences and the way mental illness is approached has sparked a deep fascination into the questions of the mind. I don't believe now that given the choice I would reverse anything I went through. In contrast, my mind is now full of questions; why is it that certain people suffer from these so-called disorders? Where and what is the line between mental illness and mental wellbeing? Can we make the distinction or is behaviour just one continuum?

As already mentioned, I have always been deeply sceptical of the diagnosis of mental disease and the labelling of certain disorders. The fact that I had to lose a certain amount of weight in a certain period of time in order to classify as 'anorexia' is a perfect example of this. Of course, the diagnosis system makes treating patients much easier, as a diagnosis allows one overall prescription to fight the label rather than treating symptoms individually. However, research into the history of psychology has highlighted to me how much time has been spent creating a reliable diagnosis system in comparison to the amount of time in developing successful methods of treatment for different and individual symptoms.

But who decides what is classed as mentally ill? Certainly, some people live with certain eccentric traits their whole lives without being diagnosed or treated. In some societies, having visions or voices speaking to them would be seen as positive and normal, coinciding with their belief system, whereas in western society this could just as easily indicate a diagnosis of schizophrenia, of having something terribly wrong with you. Historically, homosexuality was classed as a mental illness, opening up a whole host of political debate. I have come to the conclusion that a mentally ill person is someone who is seen to no longer keep up normal function in society, but this is very dependent on society itself.

I am of the opinion that certain people have certain characteristics or personality traits that leave them vulnerable to certain behaviour patterns if triggered. It is clear to see that many famous creative types, artists, composers, scientists, authors, have been known to suffer from various disorders, be it schizophrenia or manic depression. Were these people suffering from mental illnesses or did their thought processes simply not fit in with societies' view of normal? Again, from reading around the subject, I have discovered tangible links between developed society and the number of cases of mental illness. In less-developed countries, the number of reported cases of mental illness is significantly lower, and not only that, but there is a much higher recovery rate from periods of instability in less developed countries. In Britain there is a proportionally high percentage of Afro-Caribbeans diagnosed with mental illness compared with those with other cultural backgrounds. Studies have shown that Afro-Caribbean migrants rather than those born in Britain have a higher chance again of developing mental instability, yet when studying this particular race in their ethnic society, there is a very low percentage of sufferers.

For me, this research illustrates that perhaps mental illness is an individual's mechanism for coping with the stresses of society. As life in underdeveloped countries is closer to how we would have lived in primal times, I question whether it is today's society that our brains are unsuited to. Instead of being preoccupied with basic survival needs, our brains are constantly bombarded with other messages. Anorexia is a basic example of this; we are constantly surrounded by images of how we 'should' look and be; it seems to me perfectly understandable that for people with a certain personality trait, this could trigger inappropriate messages throughout the brain and an illness could be manifested in this way. What would start out as a way of dealing with what society shows us could easily become out of control if we are that way inclined or particularly vulnerable. For me, I know that I was at a particularly vulnerable stage: entering my teenage years, starting high school, unstable friendship groups; in hindsight it is easy for me to see how my illness precipitated.

I know I will always be vulnerable to becoming obsessive about certain things; however, I am able to understand my triggers now. Feelings of inadequacy and being out of control are things that can cause a stress response in me to revert back to my previous mind-set. Fortunately I can step back from these reactions to recognise them as irrational. Recently, a few people that I know of have suffered from anorexia; one girl's appearance was so shocking I had an instant reaction of jealousy perhaps. This confused me, I knew it was ridiculous, I felt deeply sympathetic towards her and wished

I could help; however the fact that I had this impulsive response reinforced my notion of personality type. I could see how certain behaviour could be almost contagious within those of a similar mind-set, almost like a competition.

Getting to the point of this spiel, the more I read about studies surrounding the global distribution of illness, the controversy over the line of normal behaviour; the more I understand why my mum's methods worked. When faced with the medical profession, I rebelled, the focus was very much on my weight, what I was eating, what exercise I could do, that when I had reached a certain weight, I would be healthy again. With my mum, these matters were irrelevant, what mattered was reprogramming the thought processes of my brain. I had got into unhealthy habits and simply needed to reverse these. Being outside was a huge help in this and supports all my hypotheses now that we function best and most logically when in the present and being where ultimately we were designed to be."

Resources

MUM PLEASE HELP
Karen Phillips

ANOREXIA NERVOSA – A SURVIVAL GUIDE FOR FAMILIES, FRIENDS AND SUFFERERS
Janet Treasure

SKILLS-BASED LEARNING FOR CARING FOR A LOVED ONE WITH AN EATING DISORDER – THE NEW MAUDSLEY METHOD
Janet Treasure, Grainne Smith and Anna Crane

EATING DISORDERS – A PARENTS' GUIDE
Rachel Bryant-Waugh and Bryan Lask

MEALTIMES AND MILESTONES
Constance Barter

THE SEVEN HABITS OF HIGHLY EFFECTIVE FAMILIES
Steven Covey

MINDFULNESS: A PRACTICAL GUIDE TO PEACE IN A FRANTIC WORLD
Prof Mark Williamson and Dr Danny Penman

WWW.THETAPPINGSOLUTION.COM
Nick Ortner gives every approachable explanation of EFT (Emotional Freedom Technique)

Printed in Great Britain
by Amazon

15787726R00089